IS THE MARKET MORAL?

THE PEW FORUM DIALOGUES ON RELIGION AND PUBLIC LIFE

E.J. DIONNE JR., JEAN BETHKE ELSHTAIN, KAYLA M. DROGOSZ

Series Editors

THE PEW FORUM
ON RELIGION
& PUBLIC LIFE

This book series is a joint project of the Pew Forum on Religion and Public Life and the Brookings Institution.

The Pew Forum (www.pewforum.org) seeks to promote a deeper understanding of how religion shapes the ideas and institutions of American society. At a time of heightened interest in religion's public role and responsibilities, the Forum bridges the worlds of scholarship, public policy, and journalism by creating a platform for research and discussion of issues at the intersection of religion and public affairs. The Forum explores how religious institutions and individuals contribute to civic life while honoring America's traditions of religious liberty and pluralism.

Based in Washington, D.C., the Forum is co-chaired by E. J. Dionne Jr., senior fellow at the Brookings Institution, and Jean Bethke Elshtain, Laura Spelman Rockefeller Professor of Social and Political Ethics at the University of Chicago. The Forum is supported by the Pew Charitable Trusts through a grant to Georgetown University.

The Pew Forum Dialogues on Religion and Public Life are short volumes that bring together the voices of scholars, journalists, and policy leaders engaged simultaneously in the religious and policy realms. The core idea behind the dialogues is a simple one: There are many authentically expert voices addressing important public questions who speak not only from their knowledge of the policy issues at stake, but also from a set of moral concerns, often shaped by their religious commitments. Our goal is to find these voices and invite them to join in dialogue.

OTHER TITLES IN THIS SERIES

Lifting Up the Poor: A Dialogue on Religion, Poverty, and Welfare Reform
Mary Jo Bane and Lawrence M. Mead

Liberty and Power: A Dialogue on Religion and U.S. Foreign Policy in an Unjust World (forthcoming)
J. Bryan Hehir, Michael Walzer, Louise Richardson, Shibley Telhami, Charles Krauthammer, and James Lindsay

One Electorate under God? A Dialogue on Religion and American Politics (forthcoming)
Mario Cuomo, Mark Souder, and others

Is the Market Moral?

A Dialogue on Religion, Economics, and Justice

Rebecca M. Blank

William McGurn

BROOKINGS INSTITUTION PRESS
Washington, D.C.

Copyright © 2004

THE BROOKINGS INSTITUTION

GEORGETOWN UNIVERSITY

All rights reserved. No part of this publication may be reproduced or transmitted in any form or by any means without permission in writing from the Brookings Institution Press, 1775 Massachusetts Avenue, N.W., Washington, D.C. 20036 (fax: 202/797-6195 or e-mail: permissions@brookings.edu).

Library of Congress Cataloging-in-Publication data
Blank, Rebecca M.
   Is the market moral? : a dialogue on religion, economics, and justice
/ Rebecca M. Blank, William McGurn.
       p.   cm. — (The Pew Forum dialogues on religion and public life)
Includes bibliographical references and index.
   ISBN 0-8157-1021-6 (pbk.)
   1. Economics—Religious aspects—Christianity.   I. McGurn, William.
II. Title.   III. Series.
BR115.E3B58 2004
261.8'5—dc22   2003023299

2 4 6 8 9 7 5 3 1
The paper used in this publication meets minimum requirements of the American National Standard for Information Sciences—Permanence of Paper for Printed Library Materials: ANSI Z39.48-1992.

Typeset in Adobe Caslon

Composition by R. Lynn Rivenbark
Macon, Georgia

Printed by Victor Graphics
Baltimore, Maryland

CONTENTS

Contents

FOREWORD

G. K. CHESTERTON writes that America is "the only nation in the world founded on a creed." He goes on to say, however, that it is also a "a nation with the soul of a church"—and that it struggles with its identity as such. Just how religious commitment should relate to the operations of government and politics often has been—and perhaps for good reason often will be—a subject of controversy and debate.

In the United States, considerations of the confluence of faith and public policy are complicated and our personal conceptions of the secular or sacred nature of public life often ambiguous. Alan Wolfe, a contributor to an earlier Brookings publication, *What's God Got to Do With the American Experiment?*, got it right when he wrote that "Americans cannot make up their minds whether religion is primarily private, public, or some easy combination of the two."

Or as Jean Bethke Elshtain—an editor of this series—put it in the same volume, "Separation of church and state is one thing. Separation of religion and politics is another thing altogether. Religion and politics flow back and forth in American civil society all the time—always have, always will. How could it be otherwise?" Exactly how this happens and when raises important policy questions that the Pew Forum Dialogues on Religion and Public Life seeks to explore.

With that in mind, the Brookings Institution, in cooperation with the Pew Forum on Religion and Public Life, is pleased to publish *Is the Market Moral? A Dialogue on Religion, Economics, and Justice*. This volume, the second in the series, grapples with the new imperatives of a global economy while working in the classic tradition of political economy, which has always treated seriously the questions of morality, justice, productivity, and freedom.

"We expect churches, synagogues, and mosques to have much to say about our personal behavior," the editors tell us, "but if the discussion is about profits and losses, religious voices are supposed to fall silent." Nothing could be further from the truth. As the editors go on to say in their introduction, "It is untrue to the actual workings of any society to say that religious voices can be heard on family life, but not on the economic underpinnings of the family; on personal responsibility, but not on the responsibility of economic actors; on generosity of the spirit, but not on the corporal and economic works of mercy."

Continuing in the tradition of our first volume, *Lifting Up the Poor: A Dialogue on Religion, Poverty, and Welfare*, by Mary Jo Bane and Larry Mead, this new book encourages public discussion and debate by presenting a dialogue between two people who are clear and honest about what they believe and why they believe it. In these pages Rebecca Blank and William McGurn, both of whom are deeply committed to public policy and their personal faith, draw on their expertise in economics in considering the morality of the market.

We are pleased that Becky Blank, dean of the Gerald R. Ford School of Public Policy at the University of Michigan, is continuing her work with Brookings. She is an economist by training and was appointed a member of the Council of Economic Advisers by President Clinton, having already served as a staff economist during the first Bush administration. Blank's affiliation with us is longstanding. In 1993, she coauthored "Poverty, Income Distribution, and Growth: Are They Still Connected?" for the *Brookings Papers on Economic Activity*. She also has been involved with the Welfare Reform & Beyond initiative at Brookings and recently edited *The New World of Welfare* with Ron Haskins, a Brookings senior fellow in Economic Studies. Becky, who describes herself as "culturally Protestant in habits of mind and heart," also chaired the committee that wrote the statement *Christian Faith and Economic Life*, which was adopted by the United Church of Christ's general synod in 1989.

We also welcome Bill McGurn as a contributor to this volume. He is chief editorial writer and editorial board member of the *Wall Street Journal* and has served as senior editor of *Far Eastern Economic Review* and as *National Review*'s Washington bureau chief. McGurn—a Roman Catholic and a graduate of a Catholic university, the University of Notre Dame—is better known to some for his work in the *Wall Street Journal*, but he is also a contributor to *First Things*, a magazine edited by Father Richard John Neuhaus and published through the Institute on Religion and Public Life, whose purpose it is to "advance a religiously informed public philosophy."

Finally, we are grateful for the support of the Pew Charitable Trusts and the Pew Forum on Religion and Public Life; without them we would not have been able to do much of our work on religion and public life. The Pew Forum dialogue series is part of its recent efforts to bring policy experts and civil leaders together to discuss the relationship between faith and public policy. Two of the series editors, my colleague E. J. Dionne and Jean Bethke Elshtain, of the University of Chicago, have been in dialogue on this question for many years and together helped found and cochair the Pew Forum on Religion and Public Life. The third editor, Kayla M. Drogosz, has a deep interest in the public purposes of religion and has helped shaped this series from the beginning.

It is customary to close with a disclaimer: the opinions expressed in this volume are those of the authors alone and do not necessarily reflect the views of the Pew Forum, the Pew Charitable Trusts, or the trustees, officers, or staff of the Brookings Institution. But speaking for myself, I can say that this book is at home in the Brookings tradition and, like the volume that preceded it, *Is the Market Moral?*, goes far to open the debate on a subject wherein the lines are drawn sharply and harden quickly by combining moral seriousness with serious scholarship.

Strobe Talbott
President, Brookings Institution

December 2003
Washington, D.C.

ACKNOWLEDGMENTS

REBECCA BLANK would like to thank Cody Rockey for his excellent research assistance and to acknowledge Harlan Beckley, David Thacher, and Jordan Matsudeira for their thoughtful comments. Blank gratefully acknowledges William McGurn for his comments on earlier drafts and for joining her in dialogue. Earlier versions of these essays were presented at the Conference on Christianity and Economics at Baylor University in November 2002 and at the Seminar on Religion and Ethics, Sellinger School of Business and Management, Loyola University, Baltimore, in February 2003. Participants at both of these presentations provided useful suggestions.

William McGurn would like to thank Rebecca Blank for her healthy and robust debate. He also wishes to recognize his godson, Jimmy Lai, leader of the world's most progressive Chinese media group, who more than any other man he knows appreciates that the freer the market the more important the morals.

Blank and McGurn wish to offer special thanks to E. J. Dionne and Kayla M. Drogosz for their comments on all the drafts of their essays and for bringing the two of them together in dialogue.

Rebecca Rimel, the president of the Pew Charitable Trusts, and Luis Lugo, the director of its religion program, helped bring the Pew Forum to life and have generously supported its program—and also work on religion and public life at the Brookings Institution—not only by offering material help, but also by sharing their vision, wisdom, and good sense. They have always shown their steadfast commitment to new ventures and continue to be supportive of this project in every possible way.

The editors also are extremely grateful to Strobe Talbott, president of the Brookings Institution, for his deep and energetic commitment to this project; to Carol Graham for her leadership as director of the Brookings Governance Studies Program; to Tom Mann and Paul Light for their friendship and for doing so much to make our projects possible; to Isabel V. Sawhill for her enthusiasm and encouragement; to Christina Counselman for helping in countless ways to bring this series to life and to Katherine Moore for all she has done to help see it to print; to Bethany Hase and Robert Wooley for administrative assistance; to Staci S. Waldvogel, who was present at the creation of the forum and constantly inspires us to live up to its purposes; to Bob Faherty, the director of the Brookings Institution Press, who never, ever fails us, embracing our projects with deep intelligence and exceptional understanding; to Becky Clark and Nicole Pagano for their work in helping the world know about Blank and McGurn's work; to Janet Walker and Eileen Hughes for being gifted and patient editors; to Susan Woollen and Sese Paul Design for creating the striking covers for the dialogue series; and to Larry Converse for once again creating an attractive book design.

Finally, our deepest gratitude goes to Melissa Rogers. She served as executive director of the Pew Forum with creativity, intelligence, and insight. It is impossible to speak of any project connected to the forum without acknowledging her thoughtful—no, absolutely essential—contribution. Melissa combined exceptional knowledge with a passion for the issues that were the focus of the forum, an extraordinary commitment to fairness and openness, and a style of dealing with her colleagues—all executive directors should study it—that brought together professionalism, warmth, understanding, and a determination to see all tasks through. Nor would this dialogue series have been possible without the dedication of the forum's associate director, Sandra Stencel. Sandy's tireless efforts and countless talents, including her ability to see around corners, are brought to bear on every forum endeavor. We are blessed to work with such a patient, gracious, and gifted person.

Above all, the editors thank the authors of this book. Arguments about the market are the stuff of regular conversation on Main Street, on Wall Street, in Washington—and, yes, on cable television. But by their willingness to follow first principles all the way to their logical conclusions and their courage in being so open about their assumptions, Rebecca Blank and William McGurn have, we think, challenged debaters in all those venues to raise not only the level of their game but also the moral seriousness of their own dialogues.

IS THE MARKET MORAL?

INTRODUCTION

E. J. DIONNE JR., JEAN BETHKE ELSHTAIN,
AND KAYLA M. DROGOSZ

IN OUR DAILY newspapers, reports about religion appear a long distance away from the business pages. Religion is so often defined as a realm far removed from the concerns of "this world" that it is assumed to have little of practical value to offer on trade and commerce, wages and dividends, investment and reward. We expect churches, synagogues, and mosques to have much to say about personal behavior, about matters related to the family and sexuality, about interpersonal dealings and individual spiritual yearnings. But if the discussion is about profits and losses, religious voices are supposed to fall silent.

This view is, of course, absurd. It is untrue to history—religious traditions have always had much to teach us about the moral underpinnings of economic systems and the practical rules for making an economy good and just. It also is untrue to human nature—if religions teach us that we are supposed to be moral in all our actions, there is no special exemption for activities in the economic sphere. We are not supposed to lie, cheat, or steal, and we are supposed to love our neighbor. If such rules do not apply to economic life, they are meaningless. And it is untrue to the actual workings of any society to say that religious voices can be heard on family life, but not on the economic underpinnings of the family; on personal responsibility, but not on the responsibility of economic actors; on generosity of the spirit, but not on the corporal and economic works of mercy.

This volume is in a long tradition of argument among religious people about what it takes to make an economic system just. We chose two people with training in economics rather than theology to present this dialogue, which gives this book a cast that is wholly different from that of most books on religion and economics. To their credit, both Becky Blank and Bill McGurn acknowledge their debts to their forebears in this debate, biblical as well as contemporary, while also bringing a splendid freshness and vigor to their arguments based, in part, on the practice and implementation of economic policy.

We suspect that the debate about to unfold here bears many similarities to the arguments about economic justice that take place every day in our nation's capital, in the meeting halls of our religious institutions, in living rooms, across back fences—and yes, on talk radio and television. Yet because Blank and McGurn have agreed to an extended, rigorous, and informed debate designed to clarify differences as well as points of agreement, we are certain that they will greatly enrich not only conversations among social scientists and policymakers but all future kitchen table, classroom, and congregation debates.

This book and the Pew Forum Dialogues on Religion and Public Life, of which it is a part, are built on the idea that religion always has and always will play an important role in American public life. Religion is by no means the only factor in public policy debates. Many who come to the public square reach their conclusions on social and economic issues for practical and ethical reasons that have little or nothing to do with faith. Nonetheless, our public deliberations are more honest and more enlightening when the participants are open and reflective about the interactions between their religious convictions and their commitments in the secular realm.

This does not happen often enough. Some participants in public debates fear that they will be misunderstood if they talk too much about their faith. Many worry—understandably—that being explicit about their faith commitments will be misinterpreted as an attempt to impose their religious views on others. We therefore salute the courage of Becky Blank and Bill McGurn, as we earlier saluted the courage of Mary Jo Bane and Larry Mead, who kicked off this series with their volume *Lifting Up the Poor: A Dialogue on Religion, Poverty, and Welfare Reform*. The willingness of these authors to bring together their academic and religious experience, their respective faith traditions, and their political commitments will, we hope, provide a model of how the religious imagination can enlighten many of our political and policy debates. After all, as Blank writes in these pages, "we are both economic and spiritual creatures."

Is the Market Moral? We gave that title to this volume because that is the question we saw both authors grappling with as their dialogue went forward. Both conclude that the market is—or at least can be—moral, though McGurn reaches that conclusion with fewer qualifications and doubts. We are fully aware that some, inside the religious community and elsewhere, would give a negative answer to the question. Those who see the market as immoral worry about any system that is based on self-interest rather than on the good of the community as a whole. Such critics would prefer systems based on production for need rather than profit and on state or collective ownership of economic resources.

But we chose our dialogue partners knowing that both, in some sense, support market economics, even as they disagree sharply on the role of government in regulating market transactions and ensuring a fair distribution of the market's rewards. We did so because we believe Blank and McGurn reflect rather well the poles of the economic debate in the United States and most other countries as it is being conducted now. At this point in history, even socialist and social democratic parties accept the necessity of markets. Such parties are not seeking ways to overturn capitalism; rather, they grapple with how the market and its outcomes can be made more just.

Blank captures the ambiguities of market outcomes well when she insists that they are "not *either* good or bad; more frequently, they are *both* good and bad." She continues: "Markets can enrich the lives of some who were previously poor while excluding others; markets also can generate new jobs and encourage the development of new human talents, even while they displace or disempower others whose skills are no longer as useful."

"The role of the church," Blank writes at another point, "is not to be 'antimarket' or 'promarket,' but to be life-affirming. In those cases in which markets and incentives promote better life opportunities, the church should affirm this, but when the market limits opportunity and creates human misery, the church must call the market to judgment and open a conversation about alternative institutions and social responses to the problem."

McGurn suggests another ambiguity in market thinking, which is usually presumed to be highly individualistic. He points to "an oft-overlooked truth," namely "that a market economy presumes more than an individual; it is impossible to have a market without a network of other human beings. If that is true, the market is not just about individual performance but, even more, about relationships." At another point, McGurn offers this memorable aphorism: "Born free, capitalist man is everywhere in contract to his neighbor."

Rebecca Blank sees herself firmly rooted in mainline Protestant traditions, "culturally Protestant in habits of mind and heart." She was born into the German Evangelical and Reformed tradition. For the better part of her life she has been an active member of the United Church of Christ (UCC). She has belonged to UCC churches that were linked with the United Methodists, the American Baptist Church, and the Presbyterian Church in America. She also chaired the committee that wrote the statement *Christian Faith and Economic Life*, which was adopted by the UCC General Synod in 1989. She currently is a member of a Presbyterian congregation. Blank is an academic economist and has been both a researcher and professor for many years. She was appointed a member of the Council of Economic Advisers by President Clinton, having served on the council staff during the administration of the first President Bush. She is now dean of the Gerald R. Ford School of Public Policy at the University of Michigan with an affiliation in the department of economics. While her specialty has been the economics of the labor market, she has also branched out to work on a wide range of social policy issues.

Blank has long maintained a personal interest in the ways in which economics and religion interact, but she says she often "wince[s] at the things that theologians write about economics, many of which are strongly critical of market economics and market outcomes." While recognizing the market's many problems, she sees no alternative to the market as a means of organizing economic activity in a complex society. She finds "no inconsistency between a strong belief in the value and power of competitive markets and the belief that our economic view of the world must be shaped by more than market analysis alone."

William McGurn is the chief editorial writer for the *Wall Street Journal*. His Catholic faith has always played a central role in his political commitments. McGurn has written extensively on the relationship between capitalism and religion, in particular on how Catholicism is not only compatible with but also complemented by the market's creative impulse. In the arguments within Catholicism about capitalism—they became especially fierce when the U.S. Catholic bishops released their powerful 1986 pastoral letter on the U.S. economy—McGurn has been a staunch defender of the capitalist ethic, of the view, as he once wrote, that "the market has an inherent moral worth."[1]

McGurn joined the Dow Jones Company in 1984 and worked as an editor for both the *Asian Wall Street Journal* and the *Wall Street Journal Europe*, first in Brussels then in Hong Kong. He left the company in 1988 to take a position as the Washington bureau chief for the *National Review*, before returning to Dow Jones in 1992 as the senior editor at the *Far Eastern Economic Review*. McGurn's experiences in Hong Kong powerfully effect his views, as his essays here make clear. "There was Hong Kong," he writes, "then the epitome of colonialism and still the embodiment of what we think of as dog-eat-dog capitalism—but apparently attractive enough that even the poorest from other countries go to extraordinary lengths to get there and where almost all its denizens face tomorrow with the idea that it was destined to be better than today."

Thus do two close students of economics, two serious people of faith, grapple with what constitutes economic justice and what makes economic sense.

Making Markets Moral

Blank is a market economist, so it is not surprising that she writes: "The key question is not 'Should there be a market?' but 'What are the limits to markets as an organizing structure for economic life?'" Hers is a nuanced view of the balance between the benefits and the costs of market activity. "In many situations, self-interested and individualistic behavior is appropriate," she writes. "But as Christians, we sometimes must balance self-interested behavior with a concern for others and for the communities in which we participate."

As Blank has written elsewhere: "A commitment to economic justice necessarily implies a commitment to the redistribution of economic resources so that the poor and the dispossessed are more fully included in the economic system."[2] Blank has produced a significant body of work dealing specifically with easing poverty, but she also finds it essential to understand *why* people are poor. "Effective social responses that reflect our religious convictions," Blank concludes, "must deal in a sophisticated manner with the diversity of problems faced by our brothers and sisters who are poor."[3]

Blank challenges the view that individual decisionmaking within competitive markets should be premised only on self-interest and utility maximization—on the assumption that "producers and consumers . . . care only about themselves, not about each other." The market, then, is not by itself a fully adequate model for Christian behavior.

An essential element of Blank's argument is the importance of placing economic concerns alongside other values and needs. Market transactions are essential, but there is a danger that the economic cost/benefit thinking that dominates markets may be applied in inappropriate ways to issues of family, community, and faith. The market should not only be kept in check, but other social institutions must "speak for alternative values in civil society," which can lead to limiting the market's reach.

She sees one role for religion in championing the need for "mediating the effects of the market economy" when such effects are neither socially nor morally acceptable. Blank draws from Douglas Meeks, who argues that one of God's primary roles in the Bible is that of an economist who distributes and redistributes resources in order to promote the greater good. "God the Economist acts in history," Blank writes, "to assure that the household of God's people is a just household, where all have the resources necessary for life."[4]

Substantial government intervention often has been required simply to keep the market from running off the rails, and state-sponsored services such as welfare, subsidized housing, homeless shelters, and child labor laws reflect moral commitments—such as compassion and concern for the next generation—that the market does not take into account. In one article Blank advised that "the unique nature of the social service area, with multiple forms of overlapping market failure, provides an opportunity for effective government involvement."[5] "One can argue for government involvement," she explains in these pages, "because the market itself pays little attention to certain strongly held social values."

Calling the market to judgment, of course, is no easy task, and maintaining generous "other-interested" behavior with the stranger, orphan, and widow requires vigilance and commitment. "A virtuous economy," she writes, "is one in which both the individual behavioral norms and the government and private structures that surround markets reflect the Christian mandate to care for the poor and the disadvantaged."

"As Christians, we cannot view all choices as morally neutral," she writes. "Some choices lead us closer to God and some turn us away." "Is the economic world no more than the sum of individual actions?" she asks. "If one's faith is to infuse all parts of one's life, it is hard to argue that community has meaning in religious life but no meaning in economic life. Religious life cannot be neatly separated from daily activities."

The Catholic Ethic and The Spirit of Capitalism

In 1993 Michael Novak published *The Catholic Ethic and The Spirit of Capitalism*, and McGurn's insistence on the "convergence between Catholic social doctrine and modern economics" closely parallels Novak's arguments on the moral necessity of markets.[6] Markets are moral, McGurn argues, because they create circumstances in which individuals can act freely and command dignity and respect. They are moral also because they foster the creation of the very wealth that that allows the poor and the oppressed to be lifted up—and, more to the point, to lift themselves up.

"For the poor," McGurn writes, "the real danger is almost never markets and almost always the absence of them."

"Human beings," McGurn says, "need the freedom to work—by which they become integrated with others—as well as the freedom to make the most of what they have worked at through associating with others."

"It strikes me as not a coincidence," McGurn concludes at another point, "that the God who made thinking beings in His own image appears to have put us in a world in which our wealth and well-being depend not only on our own freedom but on that of our neighbors."

McGurn explicitly rejects the view that capitalism leads to the exploitation of labor and concentrates resources in the hands of the wealthy and privileged. On the contrary, he says, the market system allows the human person to express his or her innate creativity and intelligence through entrepreneurship, thereby "improving and adding to God's bounty on earth."[7]

McGurn does insist that "the market must be bound by a moral culture" whose most important component is the family, the primary cultivator of virtue.[8] "The only thing that can really guarantee that a market will function in a moral way (and not to its own destruction) is a properly oriented culture within which to operate. We need to obey those red lights even when no one else is there." For McGurn, theologians help us do that.

"Theologians and economists need each other," McGurn insists. "Theologians and religiously informed activists need to have some grasp of how the economy really works if their critiques are to be taken seriously. Obversely, market economists, if they are not to succumb to the same self-destructive hubris as the socialists, need a religiously informed culture to remind them that economics is made for human beings and not vice versa."

McGurn concludes that markets are, or can be, moral with fewer quibbles than Blank, but he is uncertain whether government intervention is ever the way to make them so. He thinks that Blank is insufficiently skeptical of the government's ability to make markets moral without becoming a tool for vested interests. "If I had to sum up our respective propositions," McGurn writes in these pages, "I would say that Rebecca would probably consider it naïve to think of culture as strong enough to counter powerful market forces while I deem it even more naïve to expect government, which enjoys a monopoly of force, to do it properly."

How Many Cheers for Capitalism?

We have offered here just a taste of the argument that is about to unfold in this volume. At the risk of oversimplifying, one might summarize

McGurn's view as holding that religious people, and Christians in particular, are insufficiently appreciative of capitalism's moral contribution. "When we are inclined to talk about the need for limits on the market," McGurn writes, "it is worth remembering that for the most desperate among us, it is precisely the *limits* on the market that stand in their way."

And one might summarize Blank's view as insisting that while markets are valuable, the task of religion is to nurture a critical spirit that encourages impatience with the injustices that capitalism, or any other economic system, can leave in its wake. "We in the church are called to live in the modern economy," Blank writes, "but to maintain values that may sometimes conflict with those of the market. . . . We need to think about community interests as well as individual interests, at times opting for government structures that enforce community priorities that the market may not value, such as job safety, environmental protection, or redistribution programs that provide resources for those who cannot achieve economic self-sufficiency in the market."

Religious and nonreligious people alike care about economic justice. And what is economic justice? It might be said to rest on a "social vision" well described by Father J. Bryan Hehir. It is a vision that "seeks to preserve freedom and to provide space for private initiatives and institutions," yet does so "in a way which guarantees that the basic needs of the person, every person, are met and satisfied."[9]

A demanding standard, indeed! But it also is a morally decent standard toward which all economies and societies should strive. Religious people alone will not achieve the goal Hehir sets out, but neither will it be reached if religious people choose to be indifferent to questions of economics and social justice. By inviting us into their debate, Blank and McGurn call all of us to our obligations to contemplate what a just economy would look like, and then to act on our conclusions.

Notes

1. William McGurn, "A Challenge to the American Catholic Establishment," in George Wiegel, ed., *A New World Order: John Paul II and Human Freedom* (Washington: Ethics and Public Policy Center, 1992), p. 116.

2. Rebecca Blank, *Do Justice: Linking Christian Faith and Modern Economic Life* (Cleveland: United Church Press, 1992), p. 68.

3. Rebecca Blank, "Poverty and Policy: The Many Faces of the Poor," in Charles R. Strain, ed., *Prophetic Visions and Economic Realities* (Grand Rapids, Mich.: Eerdmans Publishing, 1989), pp. 156–68.

4. Rebecca Blank, *Do Justice: Linking Christian Faith and Modern Economic Life*, p. 18.

5. Rebecca Blank, "When Can Public Policy Makers Rely on Private Markets? The Effective Provision of Social Services," *Economic Journal*, vol. 110, no. 462 (March 2000), pp. C34–C49.

6. William McGurn, *Wall Street Journal*, Eastern ed., March 20, 1996, p. A14.

7. William McGurn, "Pulpit Economics: Christianity and Capitalism," *First Things* (April 2002), pp. 21–25. The article was adapted from an O'Hara Lecture on Business Ethics delivered at the University of Notre Dame.

8. William McGurn, "A Challenge to the American Catholic Establishment," p. 116.

9. J. Bryan Hehir, "Religious Ideas and Social Policy: Subsidiarity and Catholic Style of Ministry," in Mary Jo Bane, Brent Coffin and Ronald Thiemann, eds., *Who Will Provide: The Changing Role of Religion in American Welfare* (Boulder, Colo.: Westview Press, 2000), p. 118.

VIEWING THE MARKET ECONOMY
THROUGH THE LENS OF FAITH

REBECCA M. BLANK

ONE OF MY favorite hymns ends with a verse that calls on God to "bind all our lives together," to tie all humanity in a "living tether."[1] This image of living connection may have been poetic when the hymn was written 100 years ago, but it is real today. We are bound together with neighbors near and far in the living tether of a market economy that increasingly links our lives and the lives of others all around the globe. Theologians have long debated the appropriate relationship between religious faith and economic life. In a nation and a world where faith in "free markets" is a secular religion, it is crucial to understand the economic role of markets and to think about how they shape our community life and how we as individuals and as a nation should in turn shape and influence markets.

Let me be clear about my own background in approaching this question: I am an economist and a Christian. As an economist, I believe in markets. The opening and expansion of markets has been a major cause of the surge of economic growth in countries around the world, substantially reducing economic need and raising subsistence-level standards of living. At the same time, as a Christian I am frequently disturbed by the ways in which the rhetoric of markets and the assumptions of economics have come to be broadly used far outside the economic realm.

A word of introduction is perhaps in order. I come from a strong family tradition within the German Evangelical church. All of my recent ancestors were members of small German immigrant farming communities. One of my earliest childhood memories of the church is of discussions among the grown-ups over the merger of the German Evangelical and Reformed churches with the Congregational and Christian churches, which gave rise to the United Church of Christ (UCC). I have been an active UCC member through most of my life, and I chaired the committee that wrote the statement *Christian Faith and Economic Life*, which was adopted by the UCC General Synod in 1989. My interest in the intersection of faith and economics led me to write a follow-up book for use by adult education groups interested in thinking more about these issues.[2] Over the years I have belonged to UCC churches that were linked with the United Methodists, the Presbyterian Church in America, and the American Baptist Church. I married someone from the Lutheran tradition; upon our most recent move, to Michigan, our family joined a Presbyterian church. In short, my connections to mainstream Protestantism run deep. I have absorbed its faith tradition, particularly its commitment to social action and mission. I am not just a member of a Protestant church; I am culturally Protestant in habits of mind and heart that are deeply embedded in my behaviors and thoughts.

Professionally, I am a card-carrying mainstream economist, by anyone's standards. I received my Ph.D. in economics from MIT, and I have been on the faculty of the economics departments of Princeton and Northwestern universities. I am currently at the University of Michigan, serving as dean of the Gerald R. Ford School of Public Policy, with an affiliation in the department of economics. I have served as an economist in Washington, D.C., where I spent one year on the staff of the Council of Economic Advisers during the first Bush administration and returned for two years as a senior White House appointee and a member of the council in the late 1990s under President Bill Clinton. My specialty is the economics of the labor market, and I have branched out from this to work on a range of social policy issues.

My background has led to an ongoing personal interest in the ways in which economics and religion interact. I have to admit, however, that I often wince at the things that theologians write about economics, much of which is strongly critical of market economies and market outcomes. The market has many problems, and I discuss some of them in this book. But there is no viable alternative to the market as an organizing principle for an economic system in a complex society. The key question is not

"Should there be a market?" but "What are the limits to markets as an organizing structure for economic life?"

In beginning this discussion, I write as an economist, describing the economic model of the market and some of the individual behavioral assumptions that are embedded in that model. I note some of the benefits of a market-based economy, including some of the economic rewards that have resulted from the expansion of markets on a national and global scale. I also discuss some of the traditional criticisms of markets made from within the field of economics, such as those of market failure, situations in which markets fail to operate effectively.

I next contrast the behavioral assumptions of the market with the behavioral ethics of Christian theology and tradition—"good behavior" means one thing in the market and something very different in Christian theology. I discuss the implications of using "other-interest" rather than "self-interest" as a guiding principle in personal interactions and in employer-employee relations, an area in which markets and Christian teachings often collide.

I then explore the globalization of markets and of private enterprise, which has produced some very real advantages along with some difficult challenges and problems that have drawn extensive criticism and discussion within the literature on Christian social ethics. I look at the role of government in a market economy, arguing that there are a variety of justifications for government action beyond those conventionally recognized by economists. Government action often can be used to limit markets or to respond to economic needs or social values that the market itself does not recognize. Civic action also provides a way for individual Christians in a complex modern economy to demonstrate other-interest toward those with whom they have no personal connections. I comment finally on the role of the church within a market economy.

A comment on terminology is necessary. I use the term *markets*, by which I mean the process by which goods and services are produced, distributed, and sold. I resolutely stay away from the term *capitalism*, which is a broad and extremely ill-defined term that often is used to refer to an entire set of economic and political institutions and behaviors, as well as to a historical trajectory of development. This essay is, necessarily, about a much more limited concept.

The Operation of Markets

In describing the operation of markets, I write solely as an economist. I describe how competitive markets are assumed to operate and what advantages they offer. I also describe some of the standard criticisms of markets made by economists and the market interventions, typically government action, that such criticisms justify.

THE MODEL OF COMPETITIVE MARKETS

A market is a mechanism for buying and selling goods and services; it encompasses the entire set of interactions that occur when goods and services are bought and sold. The economic model of competitive markets predicts how buyers and sellers behave and how prices are determined when private, unregulated markets operate under certain assumed conditions. It matters little whether the market in question is for a physical product, a service, employment, raw materials, or highly processed goods; the same model largely applies to anything bought and sold.

Buyers and sellers come together in a market. The sellers post their prices, and the buyers decide from whom they will buy. The competition among different producers and different buyers ensures that goods are produced and sold at the lowest possible price. Producers trying to extract a higher price will be "bid down" by other producers who can sell more cheaply. Buyers acquire the goods they seek, constrained by their available income, which usually is determined by their earnings within the labor market. More marginal buyers—those with either fewer resources or less desire for a product—will not buy at all at higher prices, although they may buy a lower-quality version of the good at a lower price.[3]

This model of the competitive market process works as predicted only when certain assumptions are met. For instance, individuals are assumed to pursue only their own self-interest, with no concern for the well-being of any other actors in the market. Firms also are assumed to pursue their own self-interest, which means that they try to maximize their profits. Everyone involved is assumed to have "full information," that is, everybody knows what is being offered for sale, by whom, and at what price. Moreover, there are multiple potential buyers and sellers, so nobody gains more influence on outcomes by being bigger or more powerful than anybody else. All parties can choose what they want to buy and sell; none are coerced into buying something that they do not want or selling at an unattractive price.

The outcomes of this market process—the prices of goods and the quantities bought and sold—clearly depend on the resources that individuals bring to the market. "Resources" encompass everything from the raw materials (land, goods, and capital) that are available in the economy to individuals' education and training as well as their innate abilities and inherited wealth. Outcomes can always be improved by providing a greater endowment of resources to market participants.

The power of this market model lies in the promise that markets that meet the requirements for effective competition work best when left entirely on their own. Despite the fact that each actor is pursuing only his or her own economic self-interest to buy a good at the lowest possible price or to sell a good at the highest possible price, the market model predicts an outcome among all actors that cannot be improved on by someone else coming in and arbitrarily redistributing the product or changing the price. The market will bid prices to the lowest possible levels consistent with producers staying in business, allowing consumers maximum choice in how they spend their income. A competitive market has several specific advantages.

First, it provides *incentives for productivity*. If someone can produce a better product or a product that is just as good at a lower cost, that person can sell more and increase revenues. Hence markets often are credited with encouraging creativity and entrepreneurship, which is one reason why market economies are considered important engines of economic growth and development.

Second, a competitive market fosters *efficiency*. The producer who uses the fewest resources to produce a comparable good is the most successful. Using more resources entails higher costs, which translate into higher prices, which mean that fewer consumers will buy the good. This drive toward efficiency limits waste and uses both the human and nonhuman resources of an economy as effectively as possible. This assumes, of course, that the market for resources is operating effectively and that raw materials are priced correctly. If some raw materials, such as land or oil, are heavily subsidized or if their prices are not set in competitive markets, they will be overused by producers.

Third, a competitive market requires *no central direction or organization.* Markets work independently, by the voluntary association of consumers and producers. There is no need to "direct" the process from the outside, by government or any other organization. Indeed, if one tries to intervene in some way in an effectively functioning market, the presumption is that it will create inefficiencies or limit productivity. Hence markets are associated with *choice* and the freedom of individuals to act in their own best interest.

These advantages occur only when a market functions effectively. There are some key requirements for effective competition. A *system of laws* must be in place to enforce the contracts for prices or wages to which both parties agree, so that parties can make—and count on—binding agreements. If an employer promises to pay a new hire $10 an hour, he or she must actually pay that wage at the end of the month or face legal sanctions.

Information about product quality, availability, and price has to be readily available so that a buyer can assess whether a particular offer is good or bad. For some items, such as produce at a farmers' market, comparative quality and price are easily ascertained. For other items that are infrequently purchased or whose long-term quality and operating costs are not easily observable, there may be a role for a third party to develop a market that provides information about the performance of such items over time. The publication *Consumer Reports,* for instance, fits that niche.

No one buyer or seller can have *market power*—that is, no single entity can be so large that its behavior has a noticeable impact on price and market outcomes. If there is only one producer, then that producer has monopoly power and can sell at a higher price than in a competitive market. That reduces the well-being of all buyers.

Finally, for competitive markets to work, the *benefits and costs from the sale must be borne largely by the buyer and the seller.* If others who do not buy the good also are made better or worse off by its sale, then the price and volume of transactions will not reflect an efficient outcome. Economists often identify such situations as *externalities.* For instance, if child immunizations benefit not only the individuals who receive them but the larger community by reducing the risk of contagious disease, then a positive externality exists. In such situations, the market in immunizations will result in an immunization rate that is too low. There also are negative externalities. For example, the buyers and sellers of steel bars have no reason to consider the environmental problems that the manufacturing of the bars causes for residents who live near the price of steel bars and the price of pollution will not be internalized in the price of steel bars and the price will be too low.

If any of these requirements are not met, the result is a case of so-called market failure: the market outcome will not be entirely efficient. Realistically speaking, few markets meet all of these criteria all of the time, but in many cases the divergence from these assumptions may be minor and the competitive market model may still be a good descriptive simplification. There are clear differences among economists in their beliefs regarding how frequently markets fail. Milton Friedman (winner of the 1976 Nobel Prize in economics) argues in his classic book, *Capitalism and Freedom*, that departures from the competitive market model are rare and relatively unimportant.[4] In contrast, Joseph Stiglitz, winner of the 2001 Nobel Prize in economics, argues that market failures are pervasive.[5]

When the conditions for competitive markets are not met, often there is a role for some degree of government regulation. In fact, government regulation typically is designed to "correct" market failure to ensure that markets function competitively. For instance, the government requires the disclosure of information considered necessary for making fully informed transactions. This varies from the requirement that food products carry expiration dates to the requirement for corporate financial disclosure. The government monitors market power through antitrust laws and sometimes refuses to allow mergers among companies that together would have a significant share of the market. Government regulation often is explicitly designed to address problems resulting from externalities—for example, by establishing pollution control standards that force firms to adopt cleaner production techniques. The additional costs incurred may be added to product prices, so that the buyer also pays at least part of the pollution-abatement cost of the product.

In this model of competitive markets, *the accepted role of the government is only to enhance competition* in order to help markets function effectively.

If a specific market does not exhibit any of the market-failure problems described above, then there is no reason for government to be involved in that part of the economy.

In a market-based economy such as that of the United States, it is less common for the various levels of government to actually produce a good or service, although they regularly provide some public goods. These include highways, public schools, and national armed forces and local police forces to provide for national defense and public safety. The good provided in these cases is called a "nonexcludable public good"; that is, it is something, like national security or an effective road system, that benefits everyone in society. Private markets typically do not function effectively in providing goods like these. However, the range of public and nonexcludable goods is considered quite limited. There is ongoing debate about whether such things as the postal service or even schools ought to be at least partially privatized so that other providers can compete to offer these services more effectively.

INDIVIDUAL DECISIONMAKING WITHIN COMPETITIVE MARKETS

It is important to highlight the nature of individual decisionmaking that is assumed to occur within competitive markets. First, both producers and consumers are assumed to care only about themselves, not about each other. In short, the market model assumes *self-interest*. The only connection between a buyer and a seller in a market exchange, or between any two economic actors, is the self-interest of each. In 1776, Adam Smith, the father of modern economics, wrote: "It is not from the benevolence of the butcher, the brewer, or the baker, that we expect our dinner, but from their regard to their own interest. We address ourselves not to their humanity but to their self-love, and never talk to them of our own necessities but of their advantage."[6]

For producers and firms, serving one's self-interest means maximizing profits, given the production resources they have available and the price levels at which a product can be sold. For individual buyers, it means maximizing one's own well-being (economists call this maximizing *utility*), given one's available income—that is, making decisions so that one can buy as many desired goods as possible at the lowest possible prices. Within the labor market, it means that workers try to maximize their gains from work, given the skills and training that they bring to the labor market—that is, they want to earn as much as possible while spending as little time working as possible. To do so, they have to make choices regarding their hours of work and level of earnings.

For many daily economic transactions in a complex economy, the assumption of self-interest is surely an accurate one. Whether buying canned soup or the local newspaper, consumers decide to buy entirely on the basis of whether they want the soup or the newspaper enough to pay its stated price; that is, the decision is based on their own economic self-interest. They have no personal contact with the producer, and the producer has no personal contact with them; neither party considers any issue other than its own economic benefit. In an economy that bridges local communities, states, and nations, the market has to work effectively without personal contact between one actor and another. But the assumption that self-interest is the primary individual motivation in all economic transactions may create discomfort among Christians.

Second, the market assumes not only self-interest, but also *individual level decisionmaking*. The market is the sum total of the interactions of lots of buyers and sellers, with each buyer and seller behaving according to his or her personal motives. Personal preferences—on everything from jobs to car models—are important and determine individual economic choices. But these likes and dislikes are largely taken as given; little attention is paid to the sources of economic preferences, and little discussion occurs of the potential influence of culture or social norms on individual behavior. The focus is entirely on the individual: aggregate outcomes are the sum of individual choices, but individual choices are not influenced by aggregate outcomes.

Third, the market always assumes that *better or worse can be measured by the metric of "more" or "less."* More wealth is better. More choice is better. More goods are always better than fewer goods. The motivation for productivity and efficiency is that it produces "more" . . . more for the producer in terms of sales and wealth and more for the buyer in terms of choice of products. There is strong justification for such an assumption; in many cases, more *is* better. For poor families, "more" can mean health rather than hunger or education rather than illiteracy. For those at a higher level of income, "more" can mean the luxury of a break from work and of time spent with family on vacation or an adequate pension after retirement that allows them the option of simply not working if their energy and capacities are diminished. "More is better" often is a good assumption, particularly within the economic domain.

THE USE OF THE COMPETITIVE MARKET MODEL

The competitive market model of economic behavior assumes that individuals, acting in self-interest, come together within competitive markets. Underlying that model are assumptions about both human behavior and the nature of economic markets.

The oversimplified nature of the model is clearly recognized by economists. In fact, much of the interesting theoretical work in economics over the past two decades has moved far from competitive market models; today, the cutting edge of economic theory is concerned with modeling situations of less-than-perfect competition. There is a growing body of research on the implications of different types of market power—for instance, the power that exists when there is more than one firm, but few enough that they can exert individual market power. While this situation would be something less than a monopoly, it would not constitute a purely competitive market.[7] This research deals also with situations in which full information is consistently unavailable. In 2001, the Nobel Prize in economics went to three economists who have substantially changed economic thinking through their attention to situations of "asymmetric information,"[8] including those in which there is repeated interaction among economic actors, so that long-term bargaining and reputational effects become important.[9]

Economists understand many of the limitations of the simple market model; economic theory is not trapped in endless discussions about the joys of perfect competition. But the simple model of markets remains powerful for several reasons. First, it is easy to understand, and it has become the public reference point for discussions of markets and competition. Public discussions of economics typically accept the tenets of the competitive model: newspaper editorialists castigate government actions that interfere with markets and market efficiency; articles about corporate strategy assume full competition; individuals assume that self-interested economic behavior, on the part of themselves and their friends, is expected and accepted. The competitive model, however simple, is the lens through which many economic behaviors are viewed.

Second, a simple model that has a strong ability to predict outcomes can be very powerful, and the economic model of competitive markets has just that. Given a limited number of assumptions—I have laid them out in a few pages—this model does a very good job of predicting quite a few observed behavioral outcomes. Economic models predict price and employment levels in competitive markets; they predict what happens when various market failures occur in a market; and they predict how changes in government regulations or company rules change the behavior of individuals and markets. When the price of a good goes up, fewer people buy it. When the economic rewards of pursuing one occupation decrease, many people pursue another. When family income rises, families buy both more and better-quality goods. When taxes rise, people have less disposable income and that reduces their savings. All of these things might seem obvious, but they seem obvious only if the reader has grown up in a world in which competitive market behavior is implicitly understood and taken for granted even by those who have not studied it.

In short, despite its simplicity the economic model is amazingly effective at predicting a wide range of individual behaviors. In part for that reason, it has become the dominant behavioral model used in studying not only narrow economic issues but many types of policy analysis. Whether predicting the effects of welfare reform, of changes in regulations covering teen abortions, or of changes in military recruiting strategies, researchers frequently use economic models of behavior, in which individuals weigh personal benefits and costs and choose outcomes that maximize their own well-being.[10]

Third, the economic model of behavior has come to be applied to the making of a wide range of personal decisions. It has become commonplace to think of many noneconomic decisions as self-interested cost-benefit calculations. Ann Landers's famous response to letters from women with marital problems was always, "Are you better off with him or without him?" Implicit in that question is the presumption that each individual must consider his or her own welfare, balancing the costs and benefits to determine the right answer. Such an approach to human behavior mirrors the economic model of individual decisionmaking in competitive markets. It relies on the same embedded assumptions: individuals act out of self-interest; the individual decisionmaker is the only relevant actor; and typically, "more" is better.[11]

Measured in terms of growth and overall wealth, the U.S. market economy has been successful beyond anyone's wildest imagining over the past century, and that is true despite the fact that economic growth has been interrupted regularly by recessions and wars. The success of markets in fostering an unprecedented level of growth and development in the United States has led to the reification of markets and the market model, so that "market analysis" is applied to an increasing number of domains far from the direct sale of goods and services. If markets have worked so well in the economic realm, why should other areas of human interaction be excluded? Hence economists study the "marriage market," in potential mates, and political scientists talk about the "market" for political support and votes. Over time, the language of markets—of competition, individualism, and self-interest—has come to be applied to a much larger set of topics.

Christian Faith and Christian Behavior

This section confronts the behavioral assumptions of competitive market models with theological teachings about what constitutes "right action" among Christians. Christian theology surely recognizes the fact that human beings can be selfish and self-interested, but Christian faith calls us to be more than that whenever possible. If we accept an economic model that assumes that appropriate choices are made when individuals are self-interested, individualistic, and focused on the acquisition of more things, is doing so a validation of our worst natures and a turning away from Christian attributes? The economic model by itself is not a complete model for Christian behavior, but there are many ways in which one can be a faithful participant within a market economy.

Christian faith calls human beings to a life of love. At the center is love of God and faithfulness to God's calling, but such love necessarily must spill over and manifest itself in love of one's fellow human beings and love of creation. This suggests that some key theological elements must be missing from the market model of behavior.

First, Christian faith cares about the individual and individual well-being, but it also *calls people into community* with each other. In the absence of other individuals, a person cannot express love. Jesus is clear about the need for community: "For where two or three are gathered in my name, I am there among them" (Matthew 18:20).[12] The Christian community is defined in part by the loving concern that its members are expected to show to each other. Concern for others is as important as concern for oneself, as manifest in Christ's second great commandment, "You shall love your neighbor as yourself" (Matthew 22:39).

This implies that the community of believers is more than the just the sum of individual believers. Belief is deepened by community; community supports belief and encourages the expression of belief, which may lead in turn to deeper understanding and faith. Is the economic world different? Is the economic world no more than the sum of individual actions? If one's faith is to infuse all parts of one's life, it is hard to argue that community has meaning in religious life but no meaning in economic life. Religious life cannot be neatly separated from daily activities. This implies that as economic actors and economic decisionmakers, we must care about community as well as self.

This immediately leads to a second limitation of economic analysis as a model for Christian behavior. Among people of faith, self-interest is not an adequate principle for living. We are *called to be other-interested* as well as self-interested. To treat others as we treat ourselves means being concerned with those on the other side of our economic transactions. It means being concerned with workers who are impoverished or endangered by their work. It means being concerned when products do damage to God's creation.

For instance, Christian faith validates the possibility of self-giving love as a motivation for behavior. It is possible that one might care as deeply or more deeply about the well-being of others as about oneself. A classic example of such self-giving love is the love parents have for their children. For Christians, the model for this love is the love we receive from God, whose self-giving nature was most obviously manifest in Jesus' life and sacrificial death.

A third point of disconnection between Christianity and economic models of behavior is their assumption that more is better. Christianity affirms the value of abundance, but that abundance is *measured not by the abundance of material goods but by abundance of the Spirit.* Jesus describes his mission in John 10:10: "I came that they may have life and have it abundantly." What does abundant life mean? Again and again, the New Testament emphasizes the importance of living a faithful life, not a life filled with material goods, and warns that those who focus on material wealth will find it more difficult to be faithful. Christ makes it clear that human beings are to be judged not by their wealth but by their faith (Mark 10:17–26; Matthew 6:33; Luke 12:15–21).

Of course, in many instances the Bible also recognizes the importance of material well-being. "Abundant life" is not just a spiritual concept, for in order to have an abundant spirit one must have the resources necessary for life. Poverty is named as a social injustice in many prophetic writings. Jesus feeds people both literally and spiritually; he provides food for the 5,000 after the Sermon on the Mount, and it is a good thing (Luke 9:12–17). The key metaphor for Jesus' love becomes the eucharist, which is a public sharing of food and drink, the necessities of physical life. These passages offer little condemnation of material goods in and of themselves, recognizing instead that such goods can be used for good or for ill. The woman who pours expensive oil over Jesus' feet is not derided but praised for using it to honor Jesus (Mark 14:3–9). When a person defines his or her own value or the value of others by their level of income, that person violates the Christian message about human concern. But when a person uses material possessions in a way that sustains life and serves God, that is right use.

A fourth point of disconnection, closely related to the difference between abundant life and material goods, is the issue of choice. In the economic model, the more choices, the better—and no choices are inherently better or worse. If enough people want a particular good, someone will produce it. Belief in the value of markets leads some to argue for the libertarian position, which is that it is socially acceptable to provide any good for which there is a market. In this view, pornography is not a valid social concern as long as some people choose to buy it and others are willing to accept money to pose for the pictures. Similarly, if people wish to engage in prostitution—if some are willing to sell and others to buy—it is no one else's concern. This libertarian position is not a Christian position.

The issue for Christians is determining which choices allow for the possibility of a fuller life, one more oriented to God's intentions. *As Christians, we cannot view all choices as morally neutral.* Some choices lead us closer to God and some turn us away; we are called on to discern those that lead us closer. There are times when, out of love, we try to deny others a choice that they desire. We may support social or legal restrictions on certain choices because of the harm that we believe they can cause. In fact, it is precisely because Christians believe so deeply in the moral implications of human choice that some of the deepest arguments between Christians occur. Is abortion a choice that leads away from God? Is homosexuality such a choice? Or are there circumstances in which these choices are the right choices, leading individuals closer to God rather than further away? Because Christians are called to care—not only about their own choices but about the choices of others within their community—such debates have fractured and divided the Christian community. In sharp contrast, the libertarian economics model would indicate that if an individual believes him- or herself to be better off with a given choice, then no one else can validly say that the choice is wrong.

Finally, there is a particular economic concern to which all Christians are called, namely, *a concern for the poor.* Along with the call to be other-interested as well as self-interested and to be concerned with "right choice," we are particularly called to care for those who have greater need. Throughout the Old Testament, the prophets make it clear that societies are judged not just by whether they engage in the "right worship" of God, but also by whether they engage in just actions. In the New Testament, one of the most powerful passages is Jesus' clear directive about feeding the hungry and clothing the naked: "Truly I tell you, just as you did not do it to one of the least of these, you did not do it to me" (Matthew 25:45). The U.S. Catholic Bishops' letter on the economy referred to the "special obligation" that all members of society have to the poor and vulnerable.[13] Liberation theologians believe that one of the Bible's key messages is that God is with the poor in their struggle.[14]

Hence Christian teachings put special value on choices that enhance justice for the poor and that address their economic needs. This contrasts with the market in several ways: it gives greater value to some choices—

those that assist the poor—than others, and it calls people away from self-interest toward other-interest, where the "other" is the one in need. Unlike the market, which values people according to their resources and the productivity that they bring to the market, Christian teachings on poverty ascribe value to a group that has no resources. In fact, it is precisely *because* this group is without resources in the market that its members are valued and given a special place among Christians. At best the market ignores the poor because they are not participants, while Christianity brings them into the center of community concern.

Given the differences between Christian theology and self-maximizing economic models of behavior, how can one be a believer in market economics and a Christian at the same time? I do not consider that a very useful question. It is a bit like asking, "Given the sinfulness of human beings, how can one be Christian and human at the same time?" Our very humanness involves an ongoing tension between living in this world and not being entirely of this world, between what God wants of our lives and what we make of them. Being human means being economic actors who must participate in a larger economy that involves buying and selling within markets. In many situations, self-interested and individualistic behavior is appropriate, but as Christians we sometimes must balance self-interested behavior with a concern for others and for the communities in which we participate. We must decide what it means to be a faithful economic participant within the market economy.

Showing Other-Interest

The market's assumption of self-interested behavior is least adequate when applied to human relationships that are based on special concern and caring, such as those within families and among close friends. The primary impetus behind a friendship or a family relationship is not economic exchange, although economic exchange may be part of such relationships. These relationships are built on a connection among individuals based on some common shared history (including shared genetic endowments within families) that has created a network of mutual caring and responsibility. Ideally, personal love exists between friends and family members.

One aspect of love is that it is other-interested rather than self-interested. In loving relationships the key question is "How will this help or hurt the one I love?" rather than "How will this help or hurt me?" One of the delights of a truly loving relationship is that both parties are cared for in such a relationship, not because they look after their own needs but because they look after the needs of each other. Market-based models that emphasize self-interest and cost-benefit calculations seem inadequate to describe the behavior of an individual whose first thoughts are for the well-being of another.

For instance, one of the hallmarks of a market model is that it leads to efficiency and avoids spending unnecessary resources. In contrast, other-interest may be blatantly inefficient. One way to show one's love is to expend resources on nothing except that love; that is why the woman bathes Jesus' feet with expensive oil (Mark 14:3–9). He commends her for showing love, even while the disciples are criticizing her for wasting a precious resource that could have been sold to raise money. Similarly "inefficient" transactions happen all the time out of love: an adult child sits by a bed, holding the hand of an unconscious parent; parents engage in boringly repetitive activities solely because doing so delights their children; a friend listens for one more time to another friend's never-changing list of complaints and problems, knowing that listening will not produce any change in the situation.[15]

Some will protest that few families are without conflict, and that in most cases self-interested models are a more reasonable description of behavior, even inside families. While agreeing with these observations, I want to hold on to the claim that other-interest as well as self-interest is an important motive for our behavior. Other-interested love is a state of mind to which Christians are called. While few of us achieve it for long periods of time with large numbers of people, we do know that such love is humanly possible and can exist between individuals. We should organize our lives to nurture such possibilities. Even if self-interested models are more "realistic" in some sense, they should not be the only model we bring to relationships between individuals. The possibility of something different and something more abundant should be recognized.

Being other-interested does not imply a lack of self-interest. Healthy adults need a sense of self and an awareness of self-interest. But that should not preclude an awareness of others' needs that actively shapes one's actions and words. Other-interest can produce complex and morally difficult situations, particularly if one's responsibilities or concerns for different family members or friends come into conflict.

I do not argue that models based on self-interest are not useful in predicting and modeling individual behavior in many situations. I argue that in some realms of behavior such models are less satisfactory and that other models of behavior may be more appropriate. Particularly with regard to behavior within families and among friends, market models of self-interest and efficiency miss some key elements of motivation and behavior that are better viewed through the lens of other-interest.

Other-Interest beyond the Circle of Family and Friends?

To modern American audiences, it is hard to talk about such other-regarding behavior outside the realm of close friends and families. We have come to think of ourselves in such individualistic terms that besides family, there are few groups with which we identify and connect so strongly that our first thought is for the group and not for ourselves. In other cultures and at other times, this individualistic view of one's life would have been more unusual. It would have been more common to find people who identified their own desires closely with the desires of a larger community—a tribe, a religion, or an ethnic group. A typical modern reaction to such communities is that they must be psychologically unhealthy for their members. We immediately think of Jonestown or of the Branch Davidians, rather than of the Benedictines or the Sojourners.

Does this discussion of other-interest have any relevance for those in the developed world once it moves beyond one-on-one personal, long-term relationships? A high share of interactions in the modern world are among individuals who meet only casually or infrequently. The connection is even less direct between the many individuals who work to produce goods and the people who buy them; they rarely meet face-to-face. In short, a growing number of the interactions among people have become narrowly functional, encompassing only very limited connections.

For instance, I do not know the cashiers at the supermarket; we have no relationship except the one we enter into when I purchase my groceries and one of them calculates the amount I owe. Even if I see the same cashier every week (unlikely in a large grocery store), we may smile a bit more at each other, but we are unlikely to learn each other's names or extend the functional relationship to include other interactions. This does not, of course, excuse us from treating one another as fellow human beings—that is, with kindness, dignity, and patience. But the relationship between us is likely to remain quite narrow and limited.

My relationship is even more limited with the myriad of workers who help produce and deliver the products that I buy at the grocery store and whom I never see. My connection to these workers exists only through my purchase (or nonpurchase) of their product; there is little range for a wider relationship. For large numbers of the somewhat mindless transactions that we all must perform—from picking up shampoo at the local drugstore to buying a book over the Internet—we have neither the information, nor the time, nor the inclination to think in terms of developing a personal relationship with the producers of the product.

There are real benefits to this more impersonal economy. Consumers benefit because they are able to buy a wider range of products more quickly and efficiently and at a lower cost than they could in a world where they could buy only the products that their nearby neighbors produced. Benefits accrue as well to the producers of such products, who can sell more quickly and efficiently to a wider range of customers. Many also find benefits in the very impersonality of modern economic exchanges. The problems in one's personal life do not carry over to one's interactions with store clerks. In fact, one of the complaints about small-town life, in which store clerks and customers may have much stronger networks of connection, is that it can make it much harder to escape one's personal history.

Americans have voted with their feet to indicate that generally they prefer shopping at large grocery stores or big-box retail outlets, which provide a wide variety of goods at low prices, making shopping more efficient. It is not just clever marketing that has made Wal-Mart the largest corporation in America; Wal-Mart provides a type of shopping opportunity that many people find valuable. Yet the very anonymity of large stores can create a sense of isolation and alienation. Store managers know that customers prefer places where the clerks are friendly and where greeters appear to sincerely want to help. People desire a sense of personal connection, even in very limited functional relationships. A key to Wal-Mart's growth has been its ability to present itself as a place with friendly service as well as substantial choices and low prices.[16]

All of us are part of an increasingly global web of economic connections, in which our lives interact with the lives of workers, consumers, and producers around the world. One of the primary challenges facing modern Christians is the question of how to respond to the call to be other-interested, not just with our family, friends, and next-door neighbors, but with those included in the much broader definition of neighbor that Christ has given us. Indeed, the global economy has served to emphasize the truth of Christ's teaching that our neighbors are those in need, regardless of where they come from or what language they speak; we are connected to all other human beings as potential neighbors, regardless of who they are or where they live.

On the personal level, living a life that recognizes one's neighbors around the world can be very difficult. Some people respond by choosing a few issues, such as the environment or worker rights, and making economic choices that take into account the actions of companies on those issues. Some respond by trying to treat all person-to-person interactions—even those that are narrowly functional and very limited—with attention and concern. Others argue that one's personal relationships to friends and family are most important and focus on getting those right.

One advantage of organized civic action—either through the government or through voluntary associations—is that it can provide support and assistance to "neighbors" who are personally unknown to us. Supporting food assistance programs, low-income housing subsidies, and foreign development aid is a way to personally participate in helping people who are connected to the global economic network but whom we cannot know personally.

Living Together in the Workplace

The workplace is one of the arenas in which it often is particularly difficult to determine the appropriate balance between impersonal self-interested economic transactions and other-interested connections. The simple economic model of employment is clear: workers sell their labor in order to gain income; employers buy labor in order to produce goods or services. The labor market allows the self-interest of both groups to be satisfied. The market for human labor can be analyzed in exactly the same way that the market for machinery or for other inputs into the production process is analyzed. The economic term "human capital" has come to be broadly used to refer to the skills and abilities that workers bring into the work force, a direct parallel to "physical capital," which describes the inanimate resources used in production.

But the labor market is more complex, because it involves human interaction. Human beings are not machines. Workers' performance is affected by their motivation; they can't be "turned on" in the way that a machine is. Workers also often expect and receive more from employment than just their earnings. They spend a significant amount of time at work and inevitably build a network of human connections with their fellow workers. For many individuals, work provides a form of identity. When strangers meet, the question "Where do you work?" or "What do you do?" commonly arises. Employers also typically get more from their workers than just productive labor. They too create personal networks with those with whom they work, and their reputation is affected not just by the quality of their product but also by the way that they treat their workers.

Of course, the larger the company, the more likely it is that networks of connection exist only among subsets of workers—those in a particular job or those who work a particular shift—rather than among all employees. Hence CEOs of large companies may have connections with their senior staff but not with the retail sales force or shop-floor workers. And workers in one location will have few connections with workers in a plant or store at another location.

There is no single correct answer to how self-interest and other-interest should balance within employment relationships. Certainly self-interest is a legitimate concern for all involved. Workers need to earn an income and should make certain that they are being fully repaid for their contributions. It is legitimate for workers to be concerned about wages, work hours, and conditions of work; they have families and other commitments in their lives, and they should be given reasonable hours, a safe work environment, and fair repayment for their labor.

On the other side of the market, employers are producing a good at a certain cost, and they must make a reasonable profit in order for their business to survive. They are legitimately concerned with remaining in business and offering a high-quality and attractively priced product for sale. They should be able to demand that workers put in the hours for which they are paid and that they work with a reasonable level of effort. When technologies or consumer demands change, employers should be able to retool, retrain, or seek to employ workers with different skills.

The hard question is how to balance valid self-interest in the workplace with the Christian call to other-interest and concern for the community rather than the individual alone. In a good work environment, where people have the sense of being part of a team, other-interest is readily visible: someone stays late without extra compensation to help complete the work of a colleague who is home with a sick child; a senior person puts aside pressing work to help train a new employee; employees spend time outside of work putting together a celebration for a co-worker. When people feel valued at their jobs—personally valued as well as compensated for their work in monetary terms—often they are the most productive. Good employers and supervisors recognize that; they know that taking interest in the well-being and the career opportunities of their employees may promote their own self-interest as well.

But not all workplaces encourage such behavior. In some cases, employers treat workers as simply another input; they feel no commitment to any particular worker. The worst work situations often occur in low-wage jobs that require little training of or investment in the worker and for which there are many readily available job-seekers who can be hired to replace a current worker almost immediately. For many workers, there may be little sense of satisfaction or teamwork on their jobs. They may instead feel disparaged, overworked, or underpaid; they may be anxious about job security or unhappy with their fellow workers or their employers.[17] In other situations, business conditions may change and the company's survival may require employers to lay off workers or take away benefits that workers have come to rely on.

How should an individual's Christian faith influence his or her behavior in the workplace? Clearly the Christian call to concern for others and human connectedness demands that those at work be treated with the same degree of respect and kindness that any one of us would want to receive from our fellow employees. Exhibiting sincere concern about the well-being of fellow workers—whether peers, subordinates, or supervisors—is a key Christian demand. Fulfilling this demand can be easy in some cases and very hard in others. It may mean anything from remembering a co-worker's birthday to risking one's own job in order to express support for a worker who may be unfairly accused or mistreated.

Supervisors and employers have economic power over the lives of those whom they hire, and just as individual wealth can be used for good or for ill, so too can the power to hire, fire, and promote workers. This power entails a special responsibility for those who hold it to treat their workers as fairly and as respectfully as possible. Such responsibilities are never easy. When economic recession hits, supervisors have to decide which employees will lose their job. When merit raises are provided, supervisors have to make comparative evaluations and defend them to their employees. There is nothing "un-Christian" about engaging in such activities, but there are ways to deal even with difficult decisions and still communicate respect and concern to the workers involved.

Sometimes fulfilling these extra responsibilities demands creativity. When health care costs have risen rapidly, some companies have done a better job of designing health benefit packages that low-wage workers can still afford. When downsizing is necessary, some companies do a better job of giving workers advance notice and helping them retrain or locate other jobs. When workers face family difficulties that require them to be away from their job, some supervisors are better at trying to help them accomplish the work that needs to be done while allowing them the flexibility they need to resolve their difficulties.

It is at work that many of us are confronted most often with potential conflicts between what we are told are our economic responsibilities and what we take to be our Christian responsibilities. Balancing self-interest and other-interest in employment situations often is hard. There are no simple right answers about what constitutes appropriate behavior in difficult employment situations. But Christians are called to live out their faith at work; that means thinking hard about (and praying hard about) the demands that call places on their behavior.

The role of institutional structure and procedures within the workplace also deserves explicit mention. We are not just individuals who come together at work; often we also are part of larger institutional entities—companies, professional groups, unions, non-for-profit enterprises, and so forth. Our role as Christians cannot be limited to how we as individuals treat each other within these organizations; it must also encompass the rules that we establish for these institutional structures. Again, a particular responsibility must be borne by those who have the most influence on such institutional rules. The structure of economic institutions often creates or does not create incentives for supervisors to treat workers better, to evaluate their work more fairly, and to communicate with them more effectively about issues that affect their work lives.

An important part of such institutional structures is the monitoring and regulatory mechanisms that enforce appropriate behavior even among employers and companies that try to dodge their responsibilities. The role of government is important in enforcing nondiscriminatory and nonabusive work practices. Employers do have power over workers, and when moral suasion fails to make them recognize their responsibility to use that power wisely, then the power of government can be called on to enforce appropriate behavior.

It is possible to build work environments that encourage respect and cooperation among co-workers; it also is possible to build work environments that encourage suspicion, backbiting, personal insecurity, and stress. One reason to work toward the former rather than the latter is that a better work environment may create a more productive work force and a higher-quality product—that is to say, a more humane workplace might enhance the self-interest of employers. But even if there were *no* productivity or economic differences between companies that treat their workers well and those that do not, Christians are called to help make workplaces more livable and more humane. For instance, employers might help local community organizations offer after-work English classes to their immigrant workers, even if it does not improve their productivity. Employers might design health benefit packages in which higher-wage employees provide slightly greater subsidies for lower-wage employees, even if it takes extra work on the part of their benefit managers to set up such a program with local insurance companies. Companies might strictly enforce safety standards even when workers complain about having to comply with them. In short, the decisions made within an institution can be better or worse at responding to the Christian calling to be other-interested.

The Growth and Spread of Competitive Markets

I have focused so far on individual behavior and the role of faithful individuals within competitive markets, discussing microlevel decisionmaking. I have not talked about the aggregate effects of the adoption and spread of competitive markets or the relationship between individual market decisions and overall levels of employment or wealth. Here I briefly discuss some of the most salient of these macroeconomic issues, focusing on the international growth in competitive markets that has occurred in virtually all parts of the world. I acknowledge at the outset that the discussion is somewhat cursory. In a few pages I can touch only briefly on the issues and controversies regarding the expansion of markets and international trade.

Although individual ethics are an essential component of human relations, few among us can affect the global marketplace by our personal behavior. Yet such larger issues are important to persons of faith. The global reach of the market does not excuse Christians from faithful and concerned behavior toward others; in fact, it emphasizes the global meaning that "neighbor" must have for us. The issues raised here indicate why our concern must move beyond individual ethics to encompass the ethics and responsibilities of the institutions and organizations—both private and public—of which we are a part. This may, of course, be a particularly important responsibility for U.S. citizens, given the impact of American society and the U.S. government on the rest of the world.

Benefits from the Growth of Competitive Markets

Traditional agricultural societies often have very limited markets. Lacking the means to transport goods any distance, individual communities tend to be largely self-sufficient, and the possibilities for competition among them often are quite limited. Crops usually are grown on small plots and consumed almost entirely by the family that produces them. Trade is limited. There are few markets for labor; individuals stay in family or clan groups and share tasks; within-family roles often are determined by social and cultural norms. As an increasing number of countries have developed beyond feudal or traditional agricultural societies, the geographic reach of markets has grown. That growth has led in turn to growing attention to competition and to the efficiency and productivity that competition can promote.

This market expansion has also been fueled by expansions in trade routes and improvements in transportation technologies and long distance communication. Fewer and fewer of the goods that people consume are actually produced by their nearby neighbors, although a large share of services are still provided locally. (It is difficult to import a hair cut or a restaurant meal.) The spread of the market economy—both the widespread acceptance of competitive markets as a viable economic model and the actual geographic growth of such markets—has produced many advantages.

First, market expansion has given many individuals a *sense of choice about their economic lives.* Unlike traditional societies in which children follow the occupation and lifestyle of their parents, markets often provide incentives for young adults to prepare themselves for careers in the areas in which their own skills and interests are greatest. Similarly, many consumers have come to believe that choice in what they buy is a matter of right. They can choose the brand of their car, the taste of their breakfast cereal, or the neighborhood in which they live.

A second advantage, closely related to choice, is that the development of national and international markets has brought *increased wealth* to many individuals and societies. The United States has moved from a largely poor society of subsistence farmers to a society in which a great majority of citizens have resources that allow for substantial economic choice. The creation of markets that allow the free flow of labor and trade between regions, states, and nations has brought opportunities for income growth and wealth creation that did not exist when virtually all goods had to be locally produced and sold. To the extent that markets encourage entrepreneurship and inventiveness, they also have been important contributors to the technological changes that have fueled economic growth. Markets have been a key component of economic growth in many other nations and regions of the world as well.

Of course, economic growth depends on the development of political and social institutions as well as economic markets. For instance, economic growth in the United States is partly due to the long-term stability and openness of its government, which, among other things, has enacted laws that assure both producers and consumers that the terms of contracts can be enforced. The relatively low level of corruption in the private sector and in the U.S. government also is important, ensuring that productivity and efficiency are more likely to be rewarded. Both lack of stability and corruption in government are cited as key reasons why some other nations have not experienced the same degree of economic growth.[18]

Is Economic Growth Really a Good Thing?

There are those who claim that increases in wealth and economic choice have not brought clear benefits. In particular, some argue that the *costs of complex economic systems are too high* and not worth the gains in wealth. For instance, Wendell Berry worries about the loss of local human community as a result of the larger impersonal market economy.[19] Others have argued that the environmental costs of economic growth are too high and threaten the planet. Many of these writings promote a return to "simpler lifestyles" and—even if they are not consciously Christian—echo some of the Christian concerns that "more" is not always better and that some choices have greater moral weight than other choices.

I have sympathy with these arguments. I have already discussed some of the problems created by more global and hence more impersonal economic systems. I also take seriously the environmental problems that widespread economic growth often has caused. But I underscore the point made above that typically environmental problems have occurred because markets have *not* operated effectively: that is, instances of market failure have not been corrected and hence pollution costs have been ignored in production. In fact, some of the worst recent examples of environmental degradation occurred in the former Soviet territories under centrally planned, nonmarket economic regimes.

There are many arguments for committed Christians in rich countries to voluntarily adopt simpler lifestyles. Voluntary simplicity can be a way to communicate to our children what we most value in our lives. It can be a way to create time out of busy schedules for our family and for human connection and caring. It can provide a means of redistributing our own abundant resources with others who have not been as blessed.[20]

Yet, while I am happy to endorse the choice of those who choose to live more simply, I am skeptical of efforts to romanticize earlier economic communities. For most people throughout history, "simple living" has meant subsistence farming. My grandparents grew up in such a community. They did hard physical labor for long hours each day; for the most part, they ate what they could grow; and they had few career choices—the men inherited or scraped together money to buy land while the women married and raised children. That was the life available to them, and they found many ways to create community and find joy in life. But they had few choices. Their families always faced the threat of natural crop failure and hunger, of early death from disease and sickness, and of economic destitution if they lost their ability to work.

I cannot find much to admire about involuntary rural poverty, which was the economic reality for most individuals before markets brought about economic growth. I cannot compare the lives of my grandparents to the lives of my children without believing that economic growth has produced enormous human benefits. The ability and the wealth to make economic choices about our work and our lives allow us to use more effectively the diverse skills that we have been given as human beings by our Creator. Greater wealth provides many more individuals with the luxury of time and choice . . . time to think, time to form friendships, time to worship God and enjoy God's creation, and time to learn all that being human can mean.

Some have misused their wealth, letting it lead them into consumption-oriented and high-stress lifestyles. Others have misinterpreted wealth as a sign of special privilege and abused the power that wealth can provide. But, to move into Christian language, the fact that wealth can be a temptation leading toward sin does not suggest that wealth is inherently bad. Wealth, like other things that fall under our human control, such as our sexuality or our creative abilities, can be used for good or for evil. Our faith does not call us to avoid wealth but to make choices that use it productively to enhance community.[21]

DOES ECONOMIC GROWTH REDUCE POVERTY?

A second criticism of economic growth is that it has been uneven and that *not all populations have benefited equally* from the expansion of markets. Christians are called to be concerned about poverty. One of the promises of economic growth is that it can reduce economic need among the poor; if that is not the case, the value placed on growth must be much lower.

Economic growth typically has been viewed as a primary cause of reductions in poverty. In the United States, the rapid economic expansion of the 1960s was a primary reason behind the very large declines in poverty in that decade. The economic expansion of the 1990s also reduced poverty and increased employment opportunities for the poor.[22] The international evidence suggests that poverty has fallen most rapidly in regions where economic growth has been substantial over the last several decades.[23] In almost all nations where poverty rates have fallen permanently, economic expansion has occurred as well.

Yet even the amazing rates of economic growth and development in the United States have not abolished the problem of poverty. According to official numbers, almost 12 percent of all Americans lived below the U.S. poverty line in 2001.[24] Among single mothers with children, 25 percent are poor; among African Americans and Hispanics, more than 20 percent are poor. At the global level, the World Bank estimates that about one-fifth of the world's population lives on less than $1 per day.[25]

Many of the problems of poverty and need are not due to inherent problems with the functioning of markets, but rather to larger social problems that affect markets as well as other social institutions. Markets often are not the primary cause of those problems, although markets, like other social institutions, may perpetuate and exacerbate them. For instance, within the United States some poverty is due to the *institutional and social exclusion of disadvantaged and minority groups* that permeates markets as well as other social settings. Market discrimination is only one manifestation of the long history of discrimination against and exclusion of

African Americans and Native Americans. Some U.S. poverty is due to *the number of immigrants in the population*: because immigrants often arrive with fewer formal skills than native-born residents and with limited knowledge of English, they regularly "renew" the impoverished population. In 2000, 15 percent of all poor people were first-generation immigrants. Some U.S. poverty is due to *changing patterns of family composition*. The more able-bodied adults who live together, the higher the family income. Increases in divorce and nonmarital childbearing have left a high share of families with only one adult to provide and care for the children. Market outcomes of poverty and limited opportunity reflect these underlying problems.

Even so, the market economy may be blamed for doing nothing to correct the problems; in many cases it may reinforce and worsen them. Competitive markets reward those with resources. Individuals with few skills or language problems are less productive; hence the wages they earn in the market are low. The functioning of competitive markets does little to help low-skilled individuals find the resources they need to invest in training for themselves or their children. In this sense, competitive markets can reinforce historical differences in skills and resources, whatever their cause. Extra-market—often government—resources often are needed to provide a "hand up" to low-income families so that they can improve their ability to increase their earnings.

It is clear that the way that economic growth is used can do more or less to raise the well-being of all groups in society. Increased wealth that is held by only a small number of families can result in widening inequality and encourage corruption as well as political instability. Increased wealth that is used to build public infrastructure—roads, schools, health care systems—may result in broader gains among a greater share of the population. That suggests that the institutional structure of a nation's economy and the choices of its government can help to ensure that the benefits of economic growth are spread more broadly. This is one reason to be concerned about democratization—which tends to give a greater voice in economic decisionmaking to a larger number of people—in poor countries, as well as about the structure of international assistance and foreign aid programs. The economist cares about these things out of concern for long-term economic growth. The Christian also cares because of the opportunities they afford to reduce poverty and improve the lot of neighbors who live far away.

This also suggests that economic growth is validly measured by more than just an increase in a nation's gross domestic product (GDP)—the total value of goods and services produced and sold. Increasing GDP typically is necessary to promote economic development and reduce immiseration and poverty, but indicators showing changes in educational access, health outcomes, and extreme poverty might be just as important in ensuring that economic growth is being effectively used.[26]

Does the Expanded Market Economy Increase Economic Insecurity?

The most problematic charge against the growth of world markets might be that because they encourage the invention of new technologies and new products, *competitive markets encourage economic change and hence lead to economic insecurity.* On one hand, this is an advantage of markets and a reason why they lead to expanded wealth. On the other, it is why markets lead to economic uncertainty and insecurity for workers. That uncertainty is only exacerbated by the forces that underlie economic cycles of expansion and contraction, producing some periods of expanding demand and employment and some periods of higher unemployment and lower demand.

The result is that markets also can lead to impoverishment among individuals due to changes entirely beyond their control. Highly skilled and hardworking blacksmiths became obsolete and lost their livelihood when the automobile was widely adopted. The rise in computerization has displaced some workers and forced many others to learn new skills. The growing availability of skilled factory labor in other countries has led some companies to relocate more of their production facilities abroad, meaning lost jobs for some U.S. workers.

Some people adapt easily to these economic and market changes and some do not. Some changes are harder to adapt to than others. When the U.S. steel market faced greatly increased competition from abroad in the 1980s, many steelworkers lost jobs and whole communities lost their primary source of employment. "Adapting" often meant not just finding another job in a different industry, but relocating one's family far from one's lifelong home.

But economic change also means adapting to new markets and adopting new and better technologies that often reduce prices for large numbers of consumers. The economist Joseph Schumpeter referred to this process as "creative destruction," meaning that market forces provide a constant incentive to adopt new and better technologies and to abandon obsolete practices and processes. In every one of the examples of economic pain cited above, many people realized substantial economic gains. More efficient steel production has led to lower steel prices. The rise of computers has enhanced communication and productivity and created a large number of new computer-related jobs. The loss of jobs abroad has been exceeded by job growth in the United States as companies have expanded. But new jobs often are filled by a different set of workers, and those who lost the old jobs may remain unemployed. Productivity and economic growth are enhanced, but at a cost for some workers and communities.

There is no reasonable way to eliminate economic pain. In fact, the competitive rules of markets tell us that, up to a point, some pain is necessary. Workers must be encouraged to learn new skills and find new jobs as economic demands change. However, the costs of unemployment or economic disruption associated with competitive market economies are too often dismissed by those who do not experience them.

A primary role for government is not just to make markets run more efficiently, but also to redistribute resources to those who are on the losing end of economic change and development. Ideally, such programs would assist displaced workers or impoverished communities to adapt to the changes around them. The idea is not to provide a permanent subsidy, but to provide a cushion of support and assistance that allows individuals and communities to recover from economic changes that have had a negative effect on them.

There is a long tradition of Christian concern about the issue of economic change and uncertainty. Churches from a variety of traditions have spoken out in favor of unemployment insurance, of Social Security, and of job retraining programs. Christian churches and church organizations that operate through the not-for-profit sector also have a long tradition of direct outreach programs for those left behind or hurt by the process of economic growth and change.

The Role of Government

One cannot discuss the limits to markets without discussing the role of government. In a democratic society, government—the civic voice of the community—is charged with working for the common good. This immediately raises the question of how government might effectively define "the common good" and work to achieve it. The market model defines a very specific and narrow role for government, but it is clear that citizens assign government additional responsibilities. Government often plays a particularly important role for Christians who proclaim values that sometimes conflict with the assumptions and outcomes of the market economy. The government often is seen as an instrument for implementing other social values and alleviating some of the negative effects of market economies.

As discussed, the primary role of government in a competitive market economy is to ensure that markets operate effectively. This includes establishing and maintaining an effective legal system and enforcing regulations that help to overcome various market failures so that markets can operate more efficiently. Such regulations run the gamut from requirements designed to force producers to internalize the costs of production-related pollution to the requirement that companies provide full disclosure and information to consumers about their products. The accepted role for government intervention in a market economy is to overcome market failures and to create an environment that enhances market interactions.

There are, however, at least two other valid roles for government, neither of which is recognized within the economic model of competitive markets. First, governments often explicitly limit the scope of markets, not allowing certain transactions or activities to occur. Second, governments often alter market outcomes by redistributing resources among different population groups. In both roles, governments recognize that not all markets are appropriate and that not all market outcomes are desirable. In doing so, government serves as an instrument that reflects social values and choices. Especially in a democratic society, the issues debated in government and the actions taken by government are key indicators of what the society cares about. Government actions should support the market economy when appropriate. However, there are times when government should reward and encourage values other than the values of efficiency and self-interest promoted by the market.

The Government Role in Limiting Markets

Government intervenes at times to prevent certain markets from arising, either by an outright ban on selling something (such as child pornography) or by heavy taxation or regulation to discourage use of certain products (such as tobacco). These actions typically reflect social values other than those of productivity and efficiency. Radin discusses the areas in which markets are limited as "contested commodities": government action specifically limits the complete "commodification" of particular goods or services and recognizes other, nonmarket values that argue against treating them as openly traded and freely priced market commodities.[27]

For instance, the use of child labor is forbidden in most developed societies. One could view this simply as a response to a particular market failure; if young children are sent out to work and grow up illiterate or with serious health problems, they may be less productive future workers. The "market failure" is that the social benefits of having healthy, educated children are not considered in the private market.

But there are other reasons to outlaw child labor. Society may value childhood per se and want children to be happy. This means that children should not be forced into physically arduous and abusive labor. Even if such work did not affect their future productivity in any way, we might be concerned about quality of childhood and the joy that children find in life. Because we are so clearly other-interested with regard to our own children, we may find it easy to think of other people's children with some of the same care and regard for their well-being.

Governments also may limit the sale of pornography, ban certain drugs, ban the sale of human organs or body tissue, ban prostitution, and refuse to enforce certain types of employment contracts. For instance, one cannot enforce a contract that requires an employee to work for an employer for a specified length of time; a worker always has the option of leaving. (However, the employer can enforce a contract that demands that workers repay training costs if they leave before a specified length of time.) In all of these cases, certain social values are considered more important than the value ascribed to allowing free and open operation of markets. Even though some individuals would participate in such markets and even though banning the markets limits their freedom of activity, there are thought to be compelling social arguments against allowing the markets to exist.

Government prohibitions against certain markets almost always generate controversy. There always are some people who would benefit from prohibited markets, and there are those who believe that the freedom to participate in markets is more important than the values underlying the arguments against these markets.

Another form of government intervention may limit the role of the private market by having government take responsibility for providing a good or service. In such cases goods or services are publicly rather than privately provided, as with public schools, roads, police and fire protection, and Social Security benefits. In many of these cases in the United States, there is no actual ban on private markets providing the same goods and services. For instance, some communities hire private security services, there are substantial numbers of private schools, and there are many private pension schemes.

In most cases, the argument for government provision of a service involves some form of market failure. For instance, private markets may be unable to cope with the "public" nature of the service (such as police protection), or there may be large social externalities associated with it (as with public schools). In other cases, the private market fails because the individuals who are directly affected cannot themselves make decisions. In the case of prisons or foster care institutions, the government rather than the individual becomes the decisionmaker, since both prisoners and children often are viewed as being "without agency"—that is, they are unable to make responsible decisions about their own lives. Other adults must be trusted to act in their best interest.[28]

In virtually all of the instances in which a good or service is publicly provided, the belief is that the private market would simply "get it wrong": it would fail to provide the service to the people who need it most, or the service would be inadequate. One can argue for government involvement to solve "market failures" in these cases, or one can argue for government involvement because the market itself pays little attention to certain strongly held social values.

The Government Role in Altering Market Outcomes

The government regularly alters markets in order to achieve social values other than efficiency and productivity. Some of these interventions take the form of redistribution programs designed to ensure that some people do not end up in economic need; others encourage or discourage certain behaviors that are viewed as socially desirable or undesirable. Some government redistribution is necessary simply to ensure that the legal and regulatory functions of government are financed. The tax system overrides market outcomes by taxing a share of earned income. Taxes finance government operations, and the tax system is explicit acknowledgment of society's belief that government is a necessary institution whose actions benefit society.

Redistribution programs often protect certain groups that cannot participate in markets or whose participation results in extremely low income.[29] Hence the government runs income assistance programs for the disabled and the elderly, operates the food stamp program to assist families at risk of hunger, and helps fund state welfare programs that provide income and job training to families with children. One of the strongest arguments for redistribution programs is the lack of attention that the market pays to those who cannot participate in it. Those without the ability to earn income—those who are too old, too young, or ill or disabled—must survive economically outside the market. Some of these individuals are cared for within families, but family resources may be limited or unavailable.

Redistribution programs typically result in some efficiency costs, and a great deal of economic analysis of government redistribution programs focuses on trying to document and measure the inefficiencies such programs create. For instance, income support programs can discourage work. High tax rates can reduce saving. Minimum wage programs can result in unemployment among low-productivity workers who are willing to work but whom no employer is willing to hire at the minimum wage. Dozens of such analyses, however, have not resulted in the abolishment of such programs, at least in part because despite their costs, these programs have important benefits.

Other types of redistribution programs may encourage or discourage people from participating in certain markets. For instance, the U.S. tax rules that allow homeowners to deduct mortgage interest payments from their taxable income make homeownership more affordable than it would be without such a subsidy; therefore there are more homeowners than there would be in a competitive market. On the other hand, high taxes on cigarettes are designed to discourage smoking, largely because of its health hazards.

Of course, there also are government subsidies and redistribution programs that reflect political power and increase the income of groups whose income may not be at all low. Some industries, for instance, regularly receive tax breaks or other forms of government protection that enhance their profits and probably also serve to increase the number of jobs they offer or reduce the price of their products.

A few government programs intervene even further in markets. Rather than redistributing income through tax-funded subsidy programs, these programs may actually mandate certain types of market behavior, overriding the behavior that would naturally emerge within a competitive market. An example of this is the minimum wage, which requires some employers to hire workers at or above a set wage level. The case for a minimum wage typically is based on a non-economic argument, namely, that society should encourage work and that anyone who works should earn enough to survive economically. That is very different from the market argument that wages should reflect productivity. The enforcement of minimum wage laws, which force employers to pay higher wages to less-skilled workers than they would otherwise, creates higher unemployment among low-skilled workers (an economic cost) and higher wages among those who are employed (an economic benefit) than would exist in a market without a minimum wage.

Often one reason why supporters and opponents of government redistribution programs have difficulty finding common ground is that each group typically values very different outcomes. Supporters find these programs attractive because the programs prevent certain market outcomes that they consider undesirable; opponents argue that these programs are bad because they limit the functioning of the market. Each side finds benefits precisely in what the other finds objectionable.

Government programs that limit or alter market outcomes often generate intense public disagreement. Markets are broadly viewed as effective, and the market paradigm increasingly is used as a model for behavioral decisionmaking. This inevitably leads to growing suspicion of government programs that offset markets. As long as government is merely helping markets function more effectively, its actions usually are considered acceptable; even libertarians typically agree that some government legal system is necessary.

But in a world where markets are viewed more and more as the appropriate model for human behavior and for institutional design, it can become increasingly difficult to justify government actions that overturn markets. Hence the willingness to sharply reduce welfare payments through time limits and to demand that welfare recipients participate in welfare-to-work programs may reflect a growing view that market incentives should operate even for mothers with young children. They should not become "dependent" on government; alternatively stated, they should be part of the market system of employment and income-earning workers.

Similarly, the current debate over Social Security reform includes proposals to "privatize" the Social Security program—that is, to allow individuals to invest and make decisions about their own retirement savings. Full privatization would mean eliminating the Social Security tax, which forces individuals to "save" a share of their income, and allowing them to decide for themselves whether they want to save anything at all. There are fewer calls for full privatization, since many would be left without pensions and government expenditures would increase for assistance to the elderly through other programs.

I am always surprised at how difficult it is to find an acceptable public language with which to argue the value of government and the importance of government's role in restricting and overriding market outcomes. Even candidates running for major government positions often attack government programs and call for restricting the scope of government. The tax system itself—necessary for any government functioning—is a constant target of popular discontent. Redistributive taxation (which taxes higher-income families at a higher rate than lower-income families) is criticized because it reduces saving and investment among wealthier people—that is, it limits economic growth. Individual choice and program efficiency—both provided by the private market—are viewed as dominant social values. It is difficult to argue publicly that there are other social values that should at times override choice and efficiency and that may legitimately force individuals to give up certain choices.

GOVERNMENT PROGRAMS AND CHRISTIAN OBLIGATIONS

For Christians, government programs may serve as an instrument to help support the values and responsibilities taught by their faith. The important role that the Christian faith ascribes to community suggests that Christians within a democratic society should be particularly interested in helping to define the "common good" pursued by government. Government legislation that limits the scope of markets may support values that are consistent with Christian teaching, particularly when it protects individuals from choices that might bring harm to them and others. Government programs that redistribute income and respond to economic need may directly satisfy the Christian responsibility to exhibit particular concern for the poor.

This is not a call to "theocratize" government decisionmaking. It is instead a statement about the particular ways in which Christian faith may guide individual actions in a democratic society. Our faith-based values should influence how we judge and elect political decisionmakers and whether we decide to support or oppose proposed government programs. This in no way implies that Christians will or should form a monolithic voting "bloc" within society. Many well-intentioned, faithful Christians will disagree about how to apply Christian teachings to civic life in the modern world. Faithful individuals can be equally faithful whether voting for Republicans or Democrats. Biblical teachings do not tell us how to run effective redistribution programs; they do not help us to determine whether more money should go into welfare programs or into education programs. But they do unambiguously indicate that Christians should be concerned with the problems of hunger and economic need and related issues.

Because of the complexity of the modern economic world—through our involvement in private markets and through our civic identity as Americans—we affect the lives of many neighbors in this nation and throughout the globe. When we buy cheaper clothing, produced abroad, our actions affect the workers who make it. When we elect politicians who support or oppose various international trade and aid policies, our choices affect the lives of people in other countries. When we knowingly or unknowingly buy a product from a company that pays low wages and treats its workers poorly, we add to the impoverishment of those workers.

This interconnected economic web generates interconnected responsibilities to poor families and workers throughout the world. Government actions provide us as citizens with a way to recognize and respond to those responsibilities. Supporting the implementation and operation of anti-poverty and job training programs through the government is a way to act on our Christian concern for others. Supporting U.S. development aid to poor countries is a way to recognize our own economic involvement in the development patterns of the third world. In essence, civic involvement in government decisionmaking provides an avenue through which we can better fulfill the call to be a good neighbor; government as an institution connects us to our neighbors beyond our locality and beyond our nation. This is not a connection that we can afford to ignore.

None of this suggests that all government redistribution and aid programs should be blindly supported. We are also, as a citizenry, responsible for seeing that such programs are well run and for supporting programs that are effective and terminating those that are not. It is inevitable that we will disagree with many of our neighbors, both nearby and far-away, about exactly how to define "right action" by government. But the civic arena provides a place to debate and decide such issues.

Government is not, of course, the only avenue for coordinated faithful action. Individuals within local communities can help the poor. Our churches and church-based organizations often provide assistance to both local and foreign families in need. Certainly, some individuals will find involvement in organizations like Catholic Charities, Lutheran World Relief, or Church World Service to be more satisfying than civic involvement. Such church-sponsored organizations support many good and important activities. Nonetheless, they should be viewed as complements to, not replacements for, government institutions. First, the size and scope of most church-supported organizations is very limited, and they cannot undertake the broad range of actions that a national government can. Second, many church-sponsored organizations operate in cooperation with the government, and many of their activities are at least partially funded by government dollars. For instance, 22 percent of the income of America's 100 largest charities came from government sources in the 1990s.[30] These organizations are partners with the government, not competitors.

The Christian theological emphasis on the role of community and the importance of community to the individual should influence the response of individual Christians to the role of government. The competitive market model prods individuals to be suspicious of any government actions except those within a narrowly defined set because expansion of government activity is believed to encroach on individual choice. As long as individual earnings are viewed as the private property of the earners, government efforts to tax those earnings or to mandate how they are used (such as by investing a portion in Social Security) can be considered confiscatory. That is, of course, a highly individualistic view of earnings that ignores the many ways in which the community—the institutional and social structures around the individual—makes those earnings possible.[31] Employment and earnings depend not just on individual effort but also on the legal system, the cooperation of fellow workers and employers, the reliable income of buyers, the infrastructure (from roads to the Internet) that allows business to be conducted, and the education system—which is heavily subsidized by government—that provides training. One might also list the community and government institutions that help families and individuals function, allowing them to come to their jobs ready to work productively. These social and civic institutions provide the supports necessary for stable and productive private employment. The value provided by private and public institutions and by cooperative action typically goes unrecognized in a society that focuses solely on the individual's contributions.

Certainly the church, with its well-developed theologies about the value and necessity of community, has a role to play in speaking out for alternative perspectives that value the redistributive and communal functions of government.

The Role of the Church

In a world where market rhetoric often dominates and where the market model is used to describe a growing range of human interactions, what is the role of the church? I take it as a given that the church should be an actor in secular society, although I freely acknowledge the many disagreements over which roles are appropriate for the church and which are not. I believe that the church has at least two roles in economic affairs. The first is to help faithful members think about how economic reality and Christian faith might interact. Too often churches ignore economic questions, considering them outside the church's preaching and teaching role. In part this is because of the fear that such questions will divide congregations, in part because many church professionals feel inadequately informed to address such questions.

I am not promoting the view that the church must issue proclamations about current economic issues, although some churches may of course choose to do so. I am suggesting that integrating Christian faith and economic life is crucial for anyone who wants to be a practicing Christian in modern society. Market economies raise questions that relate to deep issues of faith, as discussed above. The church needs to provide space and opportunity for people who want to explore those questions to do so.[32] The attempt to keep "separate spheres" between the church and the economy is not a faithful response. Neither Jesus nor the biblical prophets shy away from thinking about how their faith relates to their economic world, nor should we.

Second, the church as an institution needs to speak for alternative values in civil society. The church need not preach against markets, but it should hold market outcomes to the same set of judgments and faith tests to which it holds other forms of human interaction.[33] I would argue that the church needs to speak for the value of other-interested behavior in a wider array of situations, more directly challenging the prevailing secular opinion that self-interested behavior is always inevitable and often preferable. The church needs to talk realistically about how other-interested behavior may apply outside of family and close friends and what its implications might be for employers, workers, and economic institutions. The goal is not to convert all church members into entirely other-interested economic actors. As I suggest above, self-interest is a reasonable response in many situations; the question is how to balance one's self-interest and other-interest. When market values (efficiency, productivity, incentives) become core secular values, the church needs to serve as a counterweight.

It may be particularly important for the church to speak of the concept of "common good" and to recognize the importance of community to the individual. Shared values are essential in any society, and religion is a force that should help shape those values. Such values are reflected in individual behavioral norms, in voluntary community behavior (through churches and other community institutions), and in government behavior in a democratic society. More attention to social ethics can provide an alternative to market models of self-interest and can offer people a language and a framework for understanding the role of the individual within the broader community and the role of government within society.

The church's role should be to speak out against the forces that oppress and limit human potential and that stunt the expression of human love. In many traditional economies, this may require that the church speak out for the values promoted by markets—that it communicate some of the human costs of government corruption or of inefficient and bureaucratized economies. In these circumstances, the church may speak in favor of the expansion of markets and the values that are embedded in markets. But in modern market economies, the secular temptation is to give the market too much power. In this case, the church must speak more often for the values that markets do not fully incorporate.

The role of the church is not to be "antimarket" or "promarket," but to be life-affirming. In cases in which markets and incentives promote better life opportunities, the church should affirm this, but when the market limits opportunity and creates human misery, the church must call the market to judgment and open a conversation about alternative institutions and social responses to the problem. This requires developing a language and a framework that allows citizens to grasp the values that the market ignores or sidelines.

Many public roles can be assumed by faithful individuals and by the church. I fully understand that some individuals, and some churches, will be called at times to more prophetic action. There will be those whose judgment of the market is harsher than mine and whose calls for change will be more radical. This prophetic tradition is an important one within Christianity, and we must listen to those who create discomfort as closely as we listen to those who comfort us. Yet I make no apologies for the focus of this essay, which has investigated how those of us who participate in a global market economy may think about faithful behavior. For most Christians in most times and places, the question will be "How do I live my life in the economy and society in which I find myself, but in a way that reflects my faith commitments?"

I find no inconsistency between a strong belief in the value and power of competitive markets and the belief that our economic view of the world must be shaped by more than market analysis alone. The market is an amazing institution; it has provided economic sustenance and opportunity for many, many people, and it has solidified our connections with our neighbors around the globe. Yet our faith teaches us lessons that the market does not: that there are times when other-interest may be more important than self-interest, when we as a society need to respond more effectively to the human pain caused by market outcomes, and when "freedom to choose" must give way to other values.

Notes

1. "Oh God of Earth and Altar" was written by George K. Chesterton in 1906.

2. Rebecca M. Blank, *Do Justice: Linking Christian Faith and Modern Economic Life* (Cleveland: United Church Press, 1992).

3. The description of competitive markets in this section is a much condensed version of that presented in every introductory economics textbook. For instance, see William J. Baumol and Alan S. Blinder, *Economics: Principles and Policy*, 9th ed. (Mason, Ohio: Southwestern Publishing, 2002).

4. Milton Friedman, *Capitalism and Freedom* (University of Chicago Press, 1962).

5. Joseph E. Stiglitz, "Information and Change in the Paradigm in Economics," *American Economic Review*, vol. 92, no. 3 (2002), pp. 460–501.

6. Adam Smith, *An Inquiry into the Nature and Causes of the Wealth of Nations*, reprint (University of Chicago Press, 1976), pp. 26–27.

7. Frederic M. Scherer reviews this literature in *Industry Structure, Strategy, and Public Policy* (Harper Collins College Publishers, 1996).

8. See the Nobel Prize lectures of these individuals in the June 2002 issue of the *American Economic Review*, vol. 92, no. 3.

9. Robert Gibbons summarizes these models in *Game Theory for Applied Economists* (Princeton University Press, 1992).

10. See Rebecca M. Blank, "What Do Economists Have to Contribute to Policy Decision-Making?" *Quarterly Review of Economics and Finance*, vol. 42, no. 5 (2002), pp. 3–19, for a discussion of why economic models are so widely used in policy decisionmaking.

11. Elizabeth Anderson discusses the underlying assumptions in cost-benefit analysis and contrasts alternative approaches to decisionmaking in *Values and Ethics in Economics* (Harvard University Press, 1993).

12. All biblical quotes are from the New Revised Standard Version of the Bible.

13. U.S. Catholic Bishops, "Economic Justice for All: Catholic Social Teaching and the U.S. Economy," *Origins*, vol. 16, no. 24 (1986), pp. 409–55, para. 16.

14. James H. Cone, *God of the Oppressed* (Maryknoll, N.Y.: Orbis Books, 1997).

15. In *Christian Existence Today: Essays on Church, World, and Living in Between* (Grand Rapids, Mich.: Brazos Press, 2001), Stanley Hauerwas claims that Christians should never judge their actions on the basis of *effectiveness*. He gives the example of Mother Theresa ministering to the dying rather than feeding hungry children.

16. Cait Murphy, "Now That Wal-Mart Is America's Largest Corporation, the Service Economy Wears the Crown," *Fortune*, April 15, 2002, p. 94.

17. Katherine S. Newman provides a description of employment in the low-wage labor market in *No Shame in My Game: The Working Poor in the Inner City* (Vintage Books, 2000).

18. Pranab Bardhan, "Corruption and Development: A Review of the Issues," *Journal of Economic Literature*, vol. 35, no. 3 (1997), pp. 1320–46.

19. Wendell Berry, *Home Economics* (San Francisco: North Press, 1987).

20. Amitai Etzioni, in *The Monochrome Society* (Princeton University Press, 2001), chapter 3, discusses the value of "voluntary simplicity" in a non-Christian context. Ronald J. Sider, *Rich Christians in an Age of Hunger* (Downers Grove, Ill.: Intervarsity Press, 1984) provides a more radical suggestion of what voluntary simplicity might mean.

21. It is interesting that the monastic lifestyle requires that participants avoid both sexual activity and the acquisition of individual wealth. Clearly both pursuits can create particularly acute temptations to sin. In both cases, Christian teachings regarding responsible and faithful use may be particularly needed.

22. Rebecca M. Blank, "Fighting Poverty: Lessons from Recent U.S. History," *Journal of Economic Perspectives*, vol. 14, no. 2 (2000), pp. 3–19.

23. Xavier Sala-i-Martin, "The World Distribution of Income," Working Paper 8933 (Cambridge, Mass.: National Bureau of Economic Research, 2002).

24. U.S. Census Bureau, *Poverty in the United States: 2001*, Current Population Reports (2002). In 2001 the U.S. poverty line was $18,100 for a family of four.

25. World Bank, *World Development Report 2000/2001: Attacking Poverty* (Oxford University Press, 2001).

26. Amartya Sen, *Development as Freedom* (Knopf, 1999).

27. Margaret Jane Radin, *Contested Commodities* (Harvard University Press, 1996).

28. See Rebecca M. Blank, "When Can Public Policymakers Rely on Private Markets? The Effective Provision of Social Services," *Economic Journal*, vol. 110, no. 462 (2000), pp. C34–C49, for a discussion of the circumstances in which the public sector might be better able to provide a good than the private sector.

29. Elizabeth Anderson, in *Values and Ethics in Economics* (Harvard University Press, 1993), refers to these political goods as "need-regarding" versus typical market goods, which are "want-regarding."

30. Rebecca M. Blank, *It Takes a Nation: A New Agenda for Fighting Poverty* (Princeton University Press, 1997).

31. Ronald H. Preston also makes this point, in *Religion and the Ambiguities of Captialism* (Cleveland: Pilgrim Press, 1993).

32. In *In Good Company: The Church as Polis* (University of Notre Dame Press, 1995), Stanley Hauerwas claims that teaching Christian ethics is itself a form of worship.

33. Martin Marty, "On Black, White, Gray, and the Rainbow," in Michael Novak, ed., *The Denigration of Capitalism: Six Points of View* (Washington: American Enterprise Institute, 1979), notes that all economic systems are flawed and must fall under God's judgment.

MARKETS AND MORALS

WILLIAM McGURN

F EW SIGHTS are charged with as much possibility as an Asian sunrise. Seen from my old perch on Hong Kong's Pokfulam Road, dawn still reveals a view of a harbor essentially unaltered by more than a century and a half of spectacular economic expansion. Trading ships from all corners of the earth rest peacefully in its waters; tiny wooden fishing boats thread their way to and fro; off in the distance the mountaintops of China fade into the morning mist.

The prosperous enclave of today is a far cry from the "barren rock with hardly a house upon it" described by Lord Palmerston back in 1840, when the British acquired Hong Kong as a spoil of their victory over China in the First Opium War. In contrast to the picturesque languor of much of the rest of the developing world, modern Hong Kong is an energetic jumble of high-rise apartment blocks, glass skyscrapers, innumerable mom-and-pop trading companies, supersize shopping malls, and ritzy hotels.

Everywhere the city sweats with commerce: street hawkers crowd every alleyway with all manner of wares; taxis, ferries, subways, limousines, buses, trains, and planes carry the city's seven million people hither and yon; Italian, French, German, Thai, Vietnamese, American, Mexican, Cantonese, Szechuan, and Korean restaurants cater to every conceivable culinary taste; furniture shops along Queens Road East churn out custom-made rosewood and rattan living, dining, and family rooms; tailors measure, cut, and fit customers of every size, shape, and race; factories the size of a one-car garage busily fill orders for everything from plastics, pencils, and micro-chips to porcelain, housewares, and picture frames for clients in Asia, Europe, the Middle East, and the Americas, all against the backdrop of pounding jackhammers and bamboo scaffolding stretching across yet another building whose outline is just rising up from the ground. And yet it is all a product of the voluntary agreements of free citizens. As author Jan Morris puts it, "There are few places in the world where such a large pro-portion of the population is at least doing what it wants to do, where it wants to be."[1]

Today Lord Palmerston's contemptuous assessment is thrown up as one example of those historical whoppers occasionally served up by per-sons of note. In fairness to the celebrated foreign secretary, however, apart from its splendid harbor there was not a great deal to recommend Hong Kong, and were he to repeat his remarks today with regard to some other land bereft of any natural advantages, he would have most every religious activist by his side. For Hong Kong has no natural resources, an inhos-pitable climate, one of the world's most densely packed populations, and not even its own water supply. Yet Hong Kong has prospered, to the point where it has long passed Mother England in average per capita income. Hong Kong is a development success story, perhaps *the* development suc-cess story.

For this reason Hong Kong has always struck me as an especially good point from which to review Catholic social teaching on matters economic. Because it is not only Hong Kong's material success that is so striking—it is the human element that makes this performance possible, something that impresses itself immediately on almost all visitors.

The reason it strikes us, I suspect, is that though most of us are not Marxists, a century and a half of Marxist intellectual agitation has not been without its effects, to the point that when we look at markets we tend to do so through the prism of the labor versus capital construct. In Hong Kong, by contrast, one sees that in capitalism the primary relation-ship is not labor versus capital but the incredible social networks that cap-ital both creates and depends upon.

The Hong Kong Advantage

If I begin with Hong Kong, it is because in my experience almost every conversation about morals and markets begins with some statement about the limits of markets, about the dangers of "unbridled" capitalism or the like. So I would like to begin mine a little differently: I'd like to talk about the possibilities of markets, especially for the most hopeless parts of the world. While markets do have their limits (but not, as I hope to explain later, the limits that most market critics have in mind), my experience, especially in the developing world, tells me that for the poor the real danger is almost never markets and almost always the absence of them.

That becomes much clearer if markets are defined as the relationships and networks between and among human beings rather than just the goods and services that are transacted. Ironically, it is precisely this emphasis on the human element that is most conspicuously absent from religion-based critiques of capitalism.

This is not, I appreciate, the prevailing view, especially in religious circles. In the prevailing view, I have it entirely backward. Economists, after all, are the practical people, concerned not with the rightness or wrongness of actions but only with the science of them and how it affects GDP. Religious workers and theologians, by contrast, are supposed to be just the opposite, conscious that man is more than a factor of production or a belly to be fed and possessed of a dignity that cannot be measured in per capita income. All of which only confirms the counterintuitive nature of my proposition here: That when it comes to how we look at the world's poor and especially their prospects for the future, our economists and business people preach a message more charged with hope than many of our Catholic theologians or activists.

This is a lesson that came to me during nearly ten years in Asia, especially when I would compare, as I was oft inclined to do, Hong Kong with Manila. On the one hand there was Hong Kong, then the epitome of colonialism and still the embodiment of what we think of as dog-eat-dog capitalism—but apparently attractive enough that even the poorest from other countries go to extraordinary lengths to get there and where almost all its denizens face tomorrow with the idea that it was destined to be better than today. On the other hand there is the Philippines, a Christian nation that is home to some of the friendliest and hardest-working people on earth, as well as to some of the cruelest exploitation of the poor by the rich outside the former communist bloc.

It was a contradiction that in human terms is summed up by the presence of more than 100,000 Filipinas in Hong Kong, many of them women possessing university degrees, working as nursemaids to strangers' children as a means of providing for their own children back home. For all the lectures on human rights and democracy coming out of post-Marcos Manila, the brutal fact of Philippine life remains that millions of its people are forced to leave their families to do dirty work elsewhere because their homeland gives them no way to feed their families—this in a strategically located land endowed with an educated, English-speaking work force and bursting with natural resources. That the only Catholic nation in all of East Asia (at least before Timor-Leste) should be a synonym for misery, corruption, and missed chances always troubled me.

Here too is where it first struck me that perhaps economists have been unfairly maligned. Even people who know nothing else about economics know one thing: that its nickname is "the dismal science." A few more might even know that it was Thomas Carlyle who came up with the gloomy appellation. But almost no one knows that Carlyle did it in an 1849 magazine article entitled "Occasional Discourse on the Negro Question," wherein he savaged the two groups then championing the antislavery cause: market economists and evangelicals.[2] For Carlyle, blacks (and, mind you, the Irish) were subhuman, and left to their own devices (or, as Carlyle saw it, the laws of supply and demand), they would be condemned to a life of misery; what they needed for humanity's sake itself was a "beneficent whip." We might not take this seriously today, but it was taken very seriously in nineteenth-century Britain, in whose soil the social arguments about capital and markets that continue to rage today have such strong roots.

My point here is not to belabor Carlyle. In the years since there have been plenty of others who have seen economists as little more than quartermasters in the Army of Mammon, toting up their accounts oblivious to the human carnage around them. Indeed, badmouthing economists may be one of the few traditions shared by the left, right, and center. Karl Marx called them sycophants of the bourgeoisie. Edmund Burke, father of conservatism, used the word pejoratively in his *Reflections on the Revolution in France*, when he lamented that "the age of chivalry is gone; that of sophisters, economists and calculators has succeeded, and the glory of Europe is extinguished forever." More tartly, George Bernard Shaw was said to have observed that "if you laid economists end to end, you would still never reach a conclusion."

My favorite is a four-line gem whose style of verse bears the name of its author, Edmund Clerihew Bentley. I quote:

John Stuart Mill
By a mighty effort of will,
Overcame his natural bonhomie
And wrote Principles of Political Economy.

Having not so much tarnished as established the public reputation of economists, I would like now to attempt something of a restoration. Whether market economists know it or not, the ideas of wealth and capital that they champion are more spiritual than material. And whether they know it or not, the preachers who look at the world's poor and see only gloom and doom are beholden to ideas about wealth and capital that are far more materialistic than spiritual—especially when it comes to the inability to distinguish between money, which in itself is barren, and capital, which represents wherewithal and opportunity. Even Marx would never make that mistake. Maybe I should say *especially* Marx.

Let me begin with language. Of all my interactions, professional as well as personal, with economists and religious, the one that lives most vividly in my memory is of a weekend spent at a seminar, the premise of which was to put the two groups together to see what would happen. In that setting, it was presently apparent that the economists, for all their flaws, understood a whole lot more about theology and its main concepts than theologians did about even the most basic elements of business and economy. Much of the dissonance between the two groups of people was conceptual rather than ideological or political: They had no real shared vocabulary, and even many of the terms fundamental to any discussion of poverty and development—capital, freedom, competition, value—held completely different meanings for each side.

This is not to say that there were no real disagreements, that at bottom every dispute was only a misunderstanding. It is, however, to suggest that we would have had a much richer conversation had we at least attached the same meanings to the same words. Plainly, in any gathering between a group concerned with the right thing to do and another concerned with doing what works, there will be clashes. And Lord knows economists are as tempted as anyone else to overstep the bounds of their discipline and define the world solely through their own prism, which in this case means moving from the reasonable proposition that economics reflects a critical aspect of human nature to the idea that economics defines that nature entirely. Pope John Paul II quite firmly tells us that economic freedom is good, but that it is only one good and not the whole of man's freedoms. If we could extract from our religious activists even an acknowledgment as limited as that—that economic freedom is a good—it would do wonders for the poor, especially if behind the acknowledgment were some real understanding of *why* and *how* the market is good. Because how we answer what Pope Leo XIII more than a century ago called "the social question" depends largely on whether we see freedom as enhancing possibilities and solidarity or taking them away. That in turn depends on whether we have a static or dynamic view of work, the latter viewing it not simply as animal toil but as a process that at its best affords all people the opportunity to be their best.

In his own encyclical on the subject, Pope John Paul II rightly places work at the heart of the church's social teaching. Work, he suggests, is "a good thing for man—a good thing for his humanity—because through work man not only transforms nature, adapting it to his own needs, but he also achieves fulfillment as a human being."[3] Work "expresses his dignity and increases it"; it provides him with the wherewithal to have a family, and it links him with his neighbor. An economist would add that in so doing the worker also contributes to the wealth of that neighbor. The point is that at the center of work are human beings, creatures separated from the animals because they are fashioned in the image and likeness of their Creator, tasked with continuing the process of creation by applying their labor and talents to the earth bequeathed them.

In short, the Holy Father's understanding of human work is that it is something far more than brute exertion, something that involves the essence of human beings themselves. The pope speaks of this as labor. We might speak of it as easily as capital, in the sense that work becomes more human to the degree that man does not simply take the world as given but adds to it, a co-creator with his Maker. In this view, man is a soul with a mind, which, when applied to the things of the earth, leaves them improved and adds to God's bounty. When we speak of a "free market," we mean a market in which a worker does this through the voluntary exchange of goods, services, and ideas. Which further implies an oft-overlooked truth: That a market economy presumes more than an individual; it is impossible to have a market without a network of other human beings. If that is true, the market is not just about individual performance but, even more, about relationships.

But there is another model of man's relation to the earth, and it traces itself to a figure who has particular relevance for this conversation because he was both economist and preacher. This is the Reverend Thomas Malthus, whose "Essay on the Principles of Population" continues to be felt more than two centuries after it was written. Before Malthus, though conceptions of wealth may have been crude and limited, when it came to human beings, at least, nations assumed as a matter of course that the more people they had, the richer and better off they were. Post-Malthus, we have a far more debilitating assumption: that when a pig is born in China, China is the richer for it, but let a Chinese baby be born, and suddenly the nation's wealth is said to have gone down.

That is not how it is expressed, to be sure. But that is how the Malthusian calculus works. At the United Nations it is practically dogma. In sharp contrast to the Christian view of man, this one sees human beings primarily as mouths to be fed. Naturally the holders of such a view do not incline to cheerfulness. Nor do they appear to learn much from the more or less regular failures of Malthusian scares to materialize. Anyone remember Paul Ehrlich's book from the 1970s, *The Population Bomb*, which opened with this now infamous sentence: "The battle to feed all humanity is over"?

The Hong Kong where I made my home for nearly a decade was not without its own Malthusian chapter. Today Hong Kong is considered the envy of Asia, perhaps the most successful of the much-hyped Asian tiger economies. But it did not look that way back in the 1950s, when China "fell" and Hong Kong was suddenly flooded with hundreds of thousands of desperate refugees. Lacking natural resources and utterly dependent on its unpleasant motherland for basics such as water and food, the colony had deteriorated so badly that a local UN official declared that the only way for it to survive would be with massive Western aid and the resettlement of refugees elsewhere. An American newspaper proclaimed Hong Kong to be dying, and the apocalypse that author John Robbins saw was reflected in the title of his 1959 book, *Too Many Asians*. Even the British in the mid-1950s grimly entitled the lead chapter in their annual Hong Kong yearbook "A Problem of People."

Yet the apocalypse that practically everyone saw just over the horizon never came to pass. In fact, Hong Kong turned out to have been on the cusp of the greatest economic boom in its history, to the point that today it supports a population of about 7 million people—more than five times the number the government declared to be Hong Kong's optimum "carrying capacity" back in 1954. Hong Kong and China, two systems, side by side: one capitalist, one socialist; one attacked as the system of the bosses and colonial exploiters, the other invoking the name of the worker. Yet it was the so-called dog-eat-dog market economy that not only made a place for hundreds of thousands of refugees at its table but allowed them to prosper and, in so doing, to enrich not only themselves but the whole of Hong Kong society. This is what economists mean when they say that the answer to poverty does not lie in trying to slice the existing pie into ever smaller slices but in baking a bigger pie for all.

Indeed, the most pernicious part of Malthus is not the stark calculus of human beings breeding themselves into extinction—though you will find that in much of the development literature today, which always appears to be telling us that development is just another billion condoms or another billion dollars in aid away. The trap is that once we accept this view, that people are liabilities and not assets, we enter a zero-sum game in which one person's prosperity comes at another's expense. In such a context, it is not surprising that talk about profit comes to look obscene, which is precisely the logic that clouds so much of our religiously informed discussions of things economic.

Let me cite an example. It is from Bishop Rembert Weakland, speaking in 1997 at Georgetown University on the tenth anniversary of the Catholic bishops' pastoral letter on economics. In that talk Bishop Weakland cited the widening gap between poor and rich nations, the race to the bottom caused by globalization, and the poor, who, he is convinced, are paying the price for everyone else's prosperity: "One aspect is for sure in the globalization process: labor is suffering most."[4]

Bishop Weakland is not alone. One of the more popular metaphors for this point of view is Spaceship Earth. I first heard that on campus in the 1970s when I was an undergraduate. It runs like this. Imagine the planet Earth as a space capsule containing five astronauts. One of them represents the developed world. And though this astronaut accounts for only one-fifth of the capsule's population, he consumes anywhere from two-thirds to nine-tenths of its resources: food, energy, you name it. The proportions reflect the figures given in the United Nations's regular *Human Development Report*, which shows the richest fifth of humanity having, for example, 90 percent of all Internet accounts, 74 percent of all phone lines, 82 percent of all export markets, and so forth.

Now there are two ways to read this. I suspect that Bishop Weakland would read it the way I had it read to me, the way the *Human Development Report* writes it, and the way the Spaceship Earth metaphor was meant to convey it: that one astronaut was hogging up far more than his fair share. Which suggests, then, something fundamentally disordered about this wealth.

But how might an economist read it? Well, he might begin by asking whence came all those resources that this one astronaut is hogging? And using the *Human Development Report*'s same measure, he would find that the developed world produces 86 percent of the world's GDP—that is, the sum total of the measures (telephone lines, the Internet, exports, and so forth) that he is supposedly taking from the poor. In other words, in almost all cases he is consuming less than he has made. And I think an economist would go even further: rather than taking that wealth as a given and coming up with some mathematical equation for taking it away from some and redistributing it to others, he would probably be more interested in the impediments holding the other four astronauts back from being as productive as their companion.

It puts me to mind of the old saw about two shoe salesmen sent to a country only to discover that everyone there walks around barefoot. The first calls up his company headquarters and says, "Bad news: Nobody here wears shoes." The other calls his company and says, "Great news! Nobody here wears shoes." In bumping around in quite a bit of the undeveloped world, I was always struck by how optimistic the investor classes were. They had to be, to put good money into Mexico or China in the 1980s and 1990s, into Korea or Taiwan in the 1950s, 1960s, and 1970s, or into Vietnam and Nicaragua today. Yet no matter how large the risk or how unpromising the circumstances, there is always someone who sees wealth and value just waiting to be unlocked and expanded.

Markets mean many things, but primarily they mean the voluntary exchange of goods, services, labor, and capital. Globalization is simply the same process carried across borders once thought to be impregnable. I appreciate that those who are not as enamored of this process as I would point out that the motivation here owes less to the Sermon on the Mount than to the bottom line. But it ought not to be dismissed as easily as it is. In words from the Second Vatican Council that John Paul used in his own encyclical on labor, "Earthly progress must be carefully distinguished from the growth of Christ's kingdom. Nevertheless, to the extent that the former can contribute to the better ordering of human society, it is of vital concern to the Kingdom of God."[5]

In this spirit, let us look at some of the numbers. We know that about three billion people live on less than $2 a day, and that this is a scandal that cries out for our attention. But one question is never asked: What happened to the *other* three billion? As the Organisation for Economic Co-operation and Development noted, a good chunk of these people were lifted out of poverty in the last half-century by market openings and the increased trade that followed.[6]

In the lexicon of the antiglobalizers, all this has been accomplished on the backs of the poorest of the poor. But the research tells a different story. Recently two economists decided to test the numbers by studying the effects of globalization on the poorest fifth of society in eighty countries. What they found exploded most of the myths. First, and most important, they found that as average income rose, the incomes of ordinary poor people rose proportionately—which is another way of saying that growth did reach the poor, dramatically and directly. More to the point, the more open the country was to trade and investment, the better its poor did. In their words: "This is not some process of 'trickle down,' which suggests a sequencing in which the rich get richer first and eventually the benefits trickle down to the poor. The evidence, to the contrary, is that private property rights, stability and openness directly and contemporaneously create a good environment for poor households to increase their productivity and income."[7]

When the poor are separated out by country and region, moreover, astonishing patterns reveal themselves. For example, half of those who moved out of poverty within the two decades ending in the late 1990s lived in East Asia—again, in those countries that have been more open to trade and globalization. By contrast, the ones that have done the absolute worst by their poor are those that have closed themselves off to globalization, most notably in sub-Saharan Africa. When we are inclined to talk about the need for limits on the market, it is worth remembering that for the most desperate among us, it is precisely the limits on the market that stand in their way.

It is worth spending some time here on the differences between the nations that have succeeded and the nations that have not, because those differences suggest that the lessons of globalization are not quite those assumed by our Bishop Weaklands. And I don't mean to pick on him; I cite his views only because I believe them to be fairly representative. I shall again try to keep statistics to a minimum. But during my time in Asia the World Bank published a report aptly entitled *The East Asian Miracle*, which focused on the performance of the region's eight most dynamic economies: Japan, Hong Kong, South Korea, Singapore, Thailand, Taiwan, and Indonesia. Since 1960, reported the bank, these economies "have grown more than twice as fast as the rest of East Asia, roughly three times as fast as Latin America and South Asia, and five times faster than Sub-Saharan Africa. They also significantly outperformed the industrial economies and the oil-rich Middle East–North Africa region. Between 1960 and 1985, real income per capita increased more than four times in Japan and the Four Tigers and more than doubled in Southeast Asian [Newly Industrialized Nations]." And here's the kicker: "If growth were randomly distributed, there is roughly one chance in ten thousand that success would have been so regionally concentrated."[8]

Worth noting too is that most of these Asian nations, rather than seeing an increase in economic inequality, found that it was actually reduced.

Which is a long way of getting back to my starting point. If you follow the business press, where I toil, you are probably pretty familiar with this story. But if you follow the religious press, as I do as a consumer, you are still waiting for that story to break. I mean that literally.

In preparation for a talk I gave last year I did a database search of four Catholic publications: *Commonweal*, *America*, *U.S. Catholic*, and the *National Catholic Reporter* (*NCR*). Again, I do not wish to imply that these are any worse than any other publications; in many respects they are much better. I just use them as representative. So I searched for any story as far back as the database went (about 1994) for articles that contained either "globalization" or "trade" in them. The results came in at 1,163 stories. You can imagine what they said. Here are some of the headlines:

—"Nearly 1 Billion Starve while Markets Boom" (*NCR*)

—"Gumbleton says United States Has Unjust Amount of Wealth" (*NCR*)

—"Making Profit the World's Highest Law" (*NCR*)

—"A New Imperialism" (*Commonweal*)

—"Global Village or Global Pillage?" (*Commonweal*)

—"Who Pays the Price for Trade: Farmers, Workers and the Unemployed" (*Commonweal*)

—"Which Mexico Is It? Globalization Is the New Form of Slavery, Dressed in the Camouflage of the So-Called Market Economy (*America*)

—"Globalization under Siege" (*America*)

To be fair, I did unearth the occasional pearl. One man wrote a story pointing out that globalization actually helped the poor, and another plaintively argued that protectionism hurt workers and productivity helped them. But you could almost count such exceptions on one hand. And surely it is no coincidence that when I read through the two exceptions I mention above, I learned that the author of one was an economist and the other was a businessman.

Assigning blame to these publications is not what interests me. What interests me is the mind-set with which they approach these issues. There is plenty that we can criticize about economists and the conduct of business; pick up the *Wall Street Journal* and you will read a good deal of it. But the almost complete indifference within faith communities to what has been, notwithstanding its flaws and incompleteness, a shift out of poverty of historic proportions involving hundreds of millions of our brothers and sisters around the world suggests that there is something more here than just ignorance of some facts. It suggests to me that many of our religiously informed activists, writers, and leaders cannot see it, because they haven't the faintest understanding of what makes it possible.

Now, the response might be along the lines of "If we concentrate on the dark patches, it's because somebody has to." Now I'm a warts-and-all man myself. But this is warts and no all, which drains it of any context that would make the story intelligible.

Let me put this another way. I am not as conversant with the Protestant denominations. But you can read most of the Catholic press devoted to these issues—and I include the diocesan papers, the bishops' letters, the conferences, and so forth—without coming across even a glimmer of recognition that we now have a pretty good idea of what makes poor countries prosper and what keeps them impoverished. You would never know, for example, that there are factories in developing nations that are not sweatshops. That many people now have a life and opportunities that their parents only dreamed about, that more of their children are going to school, that in China, where scarcely a generation ago people had to contend with starvation, they are now eating better than they ever have in Chinese history. And you would never know that most of these countries beg for foreign investment from developed nations such as the United States, because they have learned, often through bitter experience, that this is the only way to provide jobs and bring in know how.

And the record shows clearly that billions have had their lives improved, and that these people overwhelmingly come from those countries that have most opened themselves up to world markets. Am I saying then, that the answer is to trade in the Gospel of St. Matthew for *The Wealth of Nations*? Hardly. As Pope John Paul has noted on more than one occasion, however beneficial the market may be, there are things that it does not do well, primarily because it is not supposed to do them at all—and that even when the market does the things that it does do well, it must do them in the proper environment, one that orients its work in the right direction. Indeed, precisely because the market excels at efficiency, there will ever be a need to check its tendency to extend its writ beyond the realm of things useful to human beings and start applying it to human beings themselves.

As usual, Pope John Paul II has put it clearest. Up to now I have deliberately refrained from quoting from *Centesimus Annus*, but I can hardly refrain from citing the answer he gives to the direct question of whether, with the collapse of socialism, capitalism should now be the goal:

> If by capitalism is meant economic systems which recognize the fundamental and positive role of business, the market, private property and the resulting responsibility for the means of production, as well as free creativity in the economic sector, the answer is certainly in the affirmative, even though it would perhaps be more appropriate to speak of a "business economy," "market economy," or simply "free economy." But if by "capitalism" is meant a system in which freedom in the economic sector is not circumscribed within a strong juridical framework which places it at the service of freedom in its totality, and which sees it as a particular aspect of that freedom, the core of which is ethical and religious, then the reply is certainly negative.[9]

It is impossible to define a just capitalism the way the pope does in this passage without a keen appreciation for the human dynamism at its heart. For John Paul, socialism turned out the way it did—antigrowth, antihuman, and antiworker—because it was based on a false (that is, materialistic) understanding of human nature. Which helps explain why what the pope wants to temper capitalism with is not so much regulations or policies (though some regulations or policies may be an outcome of such tempering) but the culture within which the market operates. I shall flesh out the role of culture later. But it is a culture that puts man at its heart, respectful of his God-given dignity and insistent on an understanding of labor that allows each man not only to have but to be. This would be a culture, the pope says, organized around the virtue of social solidarity.

The Capital Sins

In his classic work *Catholicism, Protestantism, and Capitalism*, one of the founders of the Italian Christian Democratic Party, Amintore Fanfani, got to the heart of the matter. "For every conception of wealth," he wrote "there are corresponding rules of conduct, which, when put into practice, determine the character of the economic actions by individuals." A few lines later, Fanfani states that "the conception of wealth will be bound up with a general outlook on the universe."[10] In both these instances Fanfani is correct. Unfortunately his own conception of wealth, which held that capitalism was by its nature repugnant to Catholicism, led him to endorse a corporatist approach whose essence was put into practice by Mussolini around the same time that Fanfani was writing.

Let me go back to my initial point: that capitalism is not so much a thing but a network of social networks, at the core of which are human beings' interactions with one another. Which is why I, like the pope, prefer the word "market" or "free market," with its human associations.

To many people, including some market advocates, the market is viewed in static terms, most usually as a vehicle of efficiency. Because so many people, consciously or unconsciously, share this assumption, it is not enough for those of us who defend the market to show, as it is relatively easy to show, that in most every place it is tried, the market improves human well-being. A recent Cato Institute report entitled *The Globalization of Human Well-Being* observes that by any measure of human progress—caloric intake, child labor, education, access to safe water, life expectancy—there have been dramatic improvements at all levels, with those at the bottom showing the most dramatic increases.[11] My guess is that we could agree on whatever material measure we wished and that, if we investigated, we would find, consistently, that where the market has been allowed to operate that measure will show improvement.

But numbers never impress, and the argument is never settled. That is because the argument against the market has not been, at least not for a long time, about its efficacy.[12] We who defend the market all too often assume that all we have to do is prove that the market works and our work is done. But the argument against the market is not that it doesn't produce prosperity but that it is fundamentally dangerous or disordered, that it "works" but, perversely, works only because it is based on greed. In other words, it's a devil's pact. And so instead of listing numbers, economic studies, and so forth, I will stick with a simple proposition: that we would think more benevolently about the "market" if we started to think of it in less materialistic terms.

I call this the first capital sin. Of the seven deadly sins listed by Pope Gregory the Great, pride comes first. These sins are called capital sins, or deadly sins, because they are not simply specific acts. They reflect larger habits and outlooks: pride, anger, lust, envy, sloth, gluttony, and greed. A person who has one of these dispositions is deemed ensnared by it.

Our economic thinking, as Fanfani intimates, likewise comes with a disposition, and if we start out viewing the market solely in materialistic terms, we are condemned to materialistic conclusions. Hence my obvious play on words. What I mean by the first capital sin is the static way that capital has traditionally been defined within the Catholic tradition. For those of us who believe that capitalism represents the opportunity that comes from interacting with other human beings—not just to be rich but in some ways to be human—the hardest thing to convey is that when we hear the word "capital" we understand it to encourage the social virtue that John Paul II calls "solidarity."

Conversely, those who are not sympathetic to markets see none of that. Capital and money are the same to them. When they hear a concept such as "property rights," they likewise view it solely in terms of "stuff," that is, defending the haves and their possessions against the have nots. Whereas the sense in which we mean property rights lies in having the independence and wherewithal necessary to sustain a life separate from the government. Even those of us who cannot afford a press have an interest in the freedom to own a press, so that we might have the option for independent news.

But this view is rare within the community of Catholic activists, which is why it comes as no surprise that they tend to view the market as an inanimate machine fueled by "profit." If, however, the pope is right and we are to believe my interpretation, the market is founded as much on tapping into the God-willed impulses within ourselves, again implying that we need other human beings for our own fulfillment. How different this is from the Culture of Death, where human beings fundamentally view other human beings as impediments to their own happiness.

So if I belabor the definition here, it is because it is such an important piece of the picture. Hernando de Soto wrote a whole book on it, called *The Mystery of Capital*. In the third chapter, he puts it this way:

Walk down most roads in the Middle East, the former Soviet Union, or Latin America, and you will see many things: houses used for shelter, parcels of land being tilled, sowed, and harvested, merchandise being bought and sold. Assets in developing and former communist countries primarily serve these immediate physical purposes. In the West, however, the same assets also lead a parallel life as capital outside the physical world. They can be used to put in motion more production by securing the interests of other parties as "collateral" for a mortgage, for example, or by assuring the supply of other forms of credit and public utilities.[13]

In other words, it is not that the poor lack assets. In Manila, Bogota, or Calcutta, the poor do own things: pigs, houses, cars, bicycles, tools, and so forth. But the owners of these things are unable to use them in any but a material sense, and when they wish to sell them they can do so only in their immediate vicinity. A Filipino with a pig can sell that pig only to people who know him or who can see the pig themselves; an Iowa farmer, by contrast, has a piece of paper that transforms that pig into capital, allowing him to exchange it anywhere in the world. Likewise the squatter in Calcutta who has built a home—however crude—cannot sell it without the proper title, and so it is useful to him only as a physical roof over his head.

As I mentioned earlier, the relationship between buyer and seller, of course, is not the love of neighbor commanded by the gospels. But it is not as far removed as we might think. In the market we at least expect to be treated decently (as opposed to, say, when we're at the division of motor vehicles). And given the increasingly desperate poverty that we see in those nations that have walled their people off from globalization, we might perhaps say that one measure of solidarity is the breaking down of structures that prevent the poor from selling the fruits of their labors to all the world—and being able to take from the world what it can give them. People talk about access to markets. In human terms, that really means giving the poor access to other human beings who might help them, to their mutual benefit.

The solidarity that this kind of market sets up gives us extraordinary freedom and security. The other day, for example, I took a flight from

New York to Los Angeles with only $10 in my pocket but with no worries. Remember years ago when people would have to shell out for traveler's checks before their trips abroad? Now ordinary Americans are able to go even overseas with a minimum amount of cash because they know that a whole network exists that enables them to get money when they need it: ATM machines, credit cards, debit cards, and so forth. Every day, for those who are lucky enough to be in these networks, it becomes easier and easier to access other people, other cultures, other markets.

In the United States, so much do we take this for granted that we can hardly see how extraordinary these benefits are and how democratic they are, in the sense of being available not only to the rich but to the Average Joe. Poor peoples, by contrast, literally live outside these networks (De Soto imagines a bell jar inside which we have all these networks but outside which it remains a jungle), and it makes their lives more difficult. Fifteen years ago I went to Afghanistan to report on the war against the Soviet Union, and I carried with me several thousand U.S. dollars in a money belt because I understood that there would be no network I could rely on. The only thing that would mean anything would be U.S. dollars. Poor people find this to be true all the time, because they lack credit cards to, say, rent cars or a credit history that enables them to buy homes, expand businesses, and so forth.

In the United States, for example, the most routine source of capital for would-be entrepreneurs is the family home. Now, generally when people buy homes, they buy them to live in. Certainly my father was no different when he bought a house for our family. Yet this was a man who put six children through private (Catholic) universities on a single salary as an FBI agent.

How did he do it? Well, in addition to the scrimping and saving and sacrifices that he and my mother made, our house turned out to be a source of capital that he could borrow against. Millions of other Americans have done the same, using the value of their homes to fund everything from their children's education to family vacations to health care and home additions. In the materialist sense, the house is just a shelter. In the market sense, however, its value can be unlocked as a source of capital.

Today we chuckle over the scholastics of the Middle Ages, who never could overcome their problem with interest. Though the full story is a great deal more complicated than that and their economic analysis far more sophisticated than they've been given credit for (their idea of a just price, for example, was the market price), the scholastics' mistake at its root was in viewing money as inherently static. The failure to appreciate the more spiritual side of money took Catholic teaching down a wrong path for centuries. Two of the great economic thinkers of the Middle Ages—St. Bernardino of Sienna and St. Antonino of Florence—illustrate the contradiction.

Let me quote a paragraph from a monograph on the two churchmen published more than forty years ago:

> In classifying money as a fungible, the scholastics assumed that it was settled. *Pecunia pecuniam non parit.* Money does not breed money. In upholding this principle, the scholastics found support not only in canon law but also in a translation or mistranslation of Aristotle. In classifying money as a fungible, the scholastics assumed that it was sterile. Strictly speaking they were right in their contention, and nobody doubts that a ten-dollar bill left in a drawer, unlike mice, will not bring forth any offspring. However, this is not the point. Money, if judiciously invested, becomes productive of wealth and income. San Bernardino contradicts himself on this point by insisting in one passage of his treatise that money is barren and admitting elsewhere that it acquires "a seminal quality by being invested in a business venture and becoming capital." In fact the same contradiction is found in Thomas Aquinas, who also at one point rejects the notion that money bears fruit and, a few lines below, compares it to seed, which, if put into the soil, will sprout and produce a crop. It is true that Thomas Acquinas denies that the productive powers of money entitle the investor to interest. Nevertheless the contradiction is there.[14]

Even Marx knew that much. In its most obvious sense, Marx noted, a table was just what it appeared to be: a physical thing, made of wood. "But so soon as it steps forth as a commodity, it is changed into something transcendent. It not only stands with its feet on the ground, but in relation to all other commodities, it stands on its head, and evolves out of its wooden brain grotesque ideas, far more wonderful than table turning ever was."[15] It is not an exact parallel, but this distinction between the physical table and the table as a commodity roughly replicates the traditional philosophical distinction between matter and form, the former representing the physical and the latter the metaphysical senses. Marx's mistake was not in understanding how a table could lead a parallel life as capital, but in his insistence on a class division that by definition excluded the proletariat from having capital.

The scholastics were not against wealth. They were well aware of the parable of the talents (and less well known, the parable of the pounds) in which the master punished the servant who did not use the talents given him to create more while the master was away. But these churchmen were also aware of strictures against interest—they called it usury—in the Old Testament. Had they but allowed the distinction between mere money and capital, a distinction they did acknowledge in other parts of their writings (such as Thomas's analogy to seed), they might have spared themselves much intellectual agony. Instead they worked themselves into furious circles trying to reconcile what they knew in their bones was legitimate activity with the biblical prohibitions on usury, here opining that anything above the principal loaned was usury, there declaring that the lender had a right to obtain his opportunity costs for what he might have made on his money had he placed it elsewhere. (The author of the aforementioned monograph notes that it was John Calvin who first distinguished between business loans, for which it was proper to charge interest, and distress loans, which should be made free of charge.)

Now, church teaching has taken interesting twists and turns in the intervening centuries. My purpose, however, is not to provide a church history. It is simply to suggest that in our day a Christian appreciation of the market's virtues is impossible without a nonmaterialistic look at its spirit. Fortunately we are not without guidance. In Pope John Paul II we have a pope with first-hand experience of both communist and Nazi societies. Surely it is no coincidence that this same pope has gone further than any of his predecessors in laying out the human and spiritual underpinnings of a just market.

Remember that it was John Paul, after all, who declared that "the fundamental error of socialism is anthropological in nature."[16] Think about that. A Pole who tasted socialism's failures in almost every sector—food, clothing, housing, services, and so forth—does not treat those failures as economic. In John Paul's hands, the economic catastrophe that Polish socialism (like all other socialisms) proved to be owed itself to a false understanding of human nature. The implication is, obversely, that an economic system that works is not one based on greed but one attuned to our true nature. That sounds almost like a tautology, but it represents a huge leap forward from the grudging and perverse way in which Catholic teaching addressed the market for most of the twentieth century: as something that succeeded because it was based on the *worst* in human nature. What few of these thinkers ever did was push this assumption to its logical conclusion: What kind of God would create a world in which our prosperity depended on the worst in our natures rather than the best?

I would go further. In John Paul's writings the line between labor and capital—the division that has bedeviled debate for more than a century—is turned on its head, because the personalism that practically defines John Paul's outlook leads him to understand that labor and capital each ultimately must be traced back to the human beings behind them. And that too can hardly be a coincidence.

In his encyclical letter *Laborem Exercens,* this is how the pope describes labor:

> The word of God's revelation is profoundly marked by the fundamental truth that man, created in the image of God, shares by his work in the activity of the Creator and that, within the limits of his own human capabilities, man in a sense continues to develop that activity, and perfects it as he advances further and further in the discovery of the resources and values contained in the whole creation."[17]

In Christian teaching human beings derive their dignity from being Imago Dei, that is, created in God's image and likeness. The pope extends this to work, to which man must devote a good part of his life. What gives work its dignity is that human beings add something of themselves to the things of the earth, in a co-creation with their Creator. Jesus himself was a carpenter.

Now consider, in *Centesimus Annus,* the pope's presentation of capital:

Whereas at one time the decisive factor of production was the land, and later capital—understood as a total complex of the instruments of production—today the decisive factor is increasingly the person, that is, one's knowledge, especially one's scientific knowledge, one's capacity for interrelated and compact organization, as well as one's ability to perceive the needs of others and to satisfy them."[18]

Elsewhere the pope says that "the wealth of the industrialized nations is based much more on this kind of ownership than on natural resources."[19] That statement, in terms of adding to Creation via the human person, sounds pretty close to what he has written about labor: the defining element is human.

In other words, capital in its fundamental sense is not money but know-how: dynamic, productive, human. It is also, not coincidentally, social, geared to meeting the needs of others. As the pope's words indicate, if the market is about anything, it is about forcing producers to go outside their own wants and preferences to try to anticipate, understand, and meet the needs of others. Certainly this can be applied to satisfying desires and feeding appetites that are unhealthy: look at pornography. But the social implication is clear. Born free, capitalist man is everywhere in contract to his neighbor.

So what does all this theorizing about the nature of capital and labor mean in the real world? Primarily it reminds us that capital does not, and cannot, exist in a vacuum. For something, even money, to become capital requires a context. That context is, by definition, both human and social.

Take a Visa card. Essentially a Visa card represents a bank's promise to pay a merchant who accepts the card. To make that possible, however, the bank makes arrangements with other banks, each of which is interlocked into a network of banks across borders, continents, and oceans. Even the wealthiest of us could never hope to create such a network as individuals. But all of us with credit or debit cards benefit from these relationships, established between and among people we do not know and will never meet.

Let's apply this to countries. The human network at the root of capitalism is much more evident by its absence. In a place like Manila, which has all sorts of restrictions on capital (usually passed under the guise of protecting Filipinos), the nation's poor are cut off from more than mere money. The limits on capital—such as who can own a retail shop, which foreign companies can set up operations, whom the state will permit to tap into its natural resources—all prevent Filipinos from unleashing their productivity. That translates into fewer jobs created, which in turn leads to hundreds of thousands of people being forced to go abroad to work in menial jobs to provide for their families. Most off all, it means that ordinary people are cut off from opportunity and networks that could help them: from the Internet, from the chance to buy and sell across borders (as the rich people in their society can do), from credit to buy a home, from the right to sell their labor to a foreign employer without having to leave the country, and so forth.

This denial of human potential can also occur in a place that we might think of as rich. Take Saudi Arabia. Whatever else their feelings toward the country, most Americans think of Saudi Arabia as a modernized Arab state. Certainly the veneer is there: the five-star hotels, the Starbucks, the McDonald's. But Saudi Arabia is a good example of a country that has money but not capital. In the 1980s, when oil money was flowing in, the Saudis boasted an average per capita income of about $28,000. That has been steadily eroding, to the point that it is now less than $8,000. Think of it this way: in scarcely twenty years the Saudis have gone from being Canada to being Mexico.

In a back-handed way, the Saudi example helps explain why money, which is static, is not enough to help people develop. Back when the petrodollars were rolling in, the Saudis spent billions on infrastructure and welfare and development projects. Notwithstanding those expenditures, the one thing Saudi Arabia never managed to develop was a wealth economy, one that rewarded initiative, that encouraged the creative labors of its citizens to build on that wealth, that valued and cultivated the know-how that John Paul speaks of as the developed world's primary resource. To the contrary, Saudi Arabia today remains essentially a Beverly Hillbillies economy: one in which people suddenly found themselves with lots of cash because they discovered oil in their backyard. When oil was scarce that was all they needed. But economies do not stand still, and as new oil deposits are discovered in Russia and technology gives us alternatives to oil, the future for a one-commodity economy looks bleak over the long run.

Or take communist societies. In South Vietnam under communist rule, capital is actually reverting to money. Because of the Vietnam war, many U.S. dollars are still circulating in that nation; in fact, dollars are much preferred to the Vietnamese currency. So all across Vietnam, these dollars are literally stuffed inside mattresses, buried under floorboards, or otherwise secreted away. For really big purchases, Vietnamese use gold, which is hoarded in much the same way. Though this hard currency can be a lifesaver for ordinary Vietnamese—giving them access to goods they would otherwise be unable to buy—the limits on its legal use guarantee a tremendous waste. In a country like the United States, that gold and those dollars would be channeled through the financial system to create more wealth. But in Vietnam they remain fallow, unable to realize even a fraction of their real potential.

These are grim places, and they have directed people toward a debilitating zero-sum or fatalistic outlook on life. Against this, the capitalist disposition is strikingly cheerful, literally putting its money on the potential of human beings, given a chance, to rise above the circumstances in which they are placed. When I was growing up, the conversations at my family's dinner table revolved around sports and politics. By contrast, I once spent an evening with the family of a good friend, an ethnic Chinese entrepreneur in Manila. It was a birthday party for the patriarch of the family.

The conversations all revolved around the opportunities around them. "Hey, Pop, did you see the lot for sale in Makati—could be an office building?" Or—"There's a new restaurant going up at the Hilton; maybe they'd be interested in good French wines from our wine shop." Or—"What do you think of changing Mama's clothing factory into one for making Christmas decorations?" I sat in awe as each sibling piped up, naturally and spontaneously, with things that they had come across in the ordinary course of their days that struck them as business opportunities.

Of money and spending they spoke not at all. It was all about capital in its finest sense, something with the transformative power to generate wealth out of almost nothing. To invest and risk one's capital is, ultimately, a sign of faith, a belief that tomorrow will be better than today.

Think of it the way a young couple envisions a beautifully restored Victorian home where everyone else sees only a run-down money pit: finding potential in even the worst of circumstances. Typically the religious-inspired solution to poverty amounts to little more than tired calls for more aid, no matter that the track record of aid— whether domestic (welfare) or international (World Bank, International Monetary Fund, U.S. Agency for International Development)—has been pretty dismal. The calls for aid, moreover, always mean other people's money. When business people come into rotten areas, by contrast, they put their own money on the line. As I mentioned earlier, that is not always easy. Back in the 1950s and 1960s it took guts and vision to invest in places like Taiwan and South Korea. But that's the market. Everywhere they go, capitalists see what might be and ask "Why not?"

Which leads me back to John Paul. John Paul is no economist. But in his encyclicals on labor, capital, and truth he has finally given us what we need: a metaphysics of the market that teaches us that capital is at once human, alive, and social.

Where Are the Guardrails?

Having tried to define an idea of the market that treats it as morally larger than some super-efficient machine, let me now, finally, turn to limits. I have saved this for the end, because understanding of the nature of the market surely must precede any notion of what a just market might look like. To my mind, the nature of the market itself precludes any idea of simply regulating it into into good behavior. For one thing, not only will that approach not work, the results of such attempts only leave people more cynical than when they started.

In some quarters, particularly libertarian ones, the idea that the market has anything to do with morals is anathema. Many of these advocates argue, with some legitimacy, that the market has a way of enforcing accountability and meting out punishment when it gets the idea that some wrong has been done. They also note that the attempts to regulate markets into good behavior often have unintended consequences that can be worse than the ills the regulations were meant to cure.

As the responses to the recent scandals in corporate America demonstrate, however, the public will simply not accept the idea of an amoral market. The fallout from Enron, Tyco, WorldCom, and so forth, has led to a fundamental re-questioning of many assumptions of modern American business life. In a painful way, for example, it has reminded us that even in the biggest companies, personal character still matters intensely, that a blue-chip name is no guarantee of honesty. Ironically, even the corporate audits intended to guarantee the integrity of a company's financial statements have now come into question, something my libertarian friends would be quick to point out as one of those unintended consequences of a government mandate.

We at the *Wall Street Journal* can hardly be taken as antibusiness or antimarket. And though we may not have the same take on these scandals as, say, the people who want to use them to block the privatization of Social Security, we take these scandals seriously. Some, after all, involve crimes. And even those actions that are not crimes can threaten the confidence of participants, upon which the system depends, especially when the participants are manipulated for political ends.

Which brings us to the key question: How? Assuming that we recognize the market as something more than a machine that spits out goods and services, how do we approach it morally without doing what so many previous reformers have so often ended up doing: killing the goose that lays the golden eggs?

Certainly John Paul II is no libertarian, and he has on more than one occasion excoriated unbridled capitalism. And here is where some of the confusion comes in. Because the pope does clearly talk about limits: limits to property rights, limits to what the market can bear, limits to the arenas in which the market is to be the arbiter. This in turn has been interpreted, incorrectly, I believe, by many as a view of the market as an efficient but voracious beast that must be caged.

Government regulation and intervention may be necessary in many parts of our lives, an outcome of socially accepted efforts to keep the market away from those areas where it overreaches. But the idea, so beloved of whole generations of Catholic intellectuals, that there is some sort of "third way" between capitalism and socialism has caused as much mischief as the scholastics' prohibitions on interest. As former Czech prime minister Vaclav Klaus likes to say, "The Third Way is the fastest way to the Third World." The assumption here is that you can, using regulation, "tame" the market into moral channels without losing any of its necessary dynamism. Whole countries are still paying for that conceit, literally.

That does not mean that we submit to a world in which the market is the end and be all of human existence. If I understand the pope correctly, the moral influence on the market that he desires ought to come from our culture. This does not get too much attention, but if there is one thing that is consistent in all John Paul's writings it is the priority of culture in society. Culture has to come first. Because the market depends on virtues—self-restraint, honesty, courage, diligence, the willingness to defer gratification—that it cannot itself create. Francis Fukuyama calls it social capital. And we depend on this social capital to allow our free society to function, even more than on our formal rules.

Let me make an analogy to traffic. In the United States tens of millions of drivers make their way to and fro each day in their personal automobiles, in traffic that is regulated by red lights, speed limits, rules for passing, and so forth. These rules, to be sure, are backed up by state force: the police issue tickets for relatively minor offenses and will arrest drivers for more serious ones, such as drunk driving. But if obedience to the rules of the game depended solely on the threat of police action, the system would break down. Anyone who has been in a third world city where the traffic system *has* broken down into anarchy knows exactly what I mean.

Certainly the threat of force will always be necessary even in the best societies, because there will always be those who will not adhere to rules unless they are forced to. Most of us, however, do not stop at a traffic light at 2:00 a.m. at a deserted crossroads because we think that the police will catch us if we don't. We wait at that red light because it is part of a habit, a culture of good driving, if you will. Pretty obviously, if our traffic system depended entirely on the police to enforce it, it would not work, because there simply are not enough police officers to go around. Somewhere in here there is a measure of trust and self-control. That is true in all human endeavor.

And that is just what the pope means by the priority of culture. Some regulation will always be necessary for men and women to exercise their freedom through the market. But however necessary that regulation is, it is far short of sufficient for the operation of a moral market. What the pope is saying is more like the traffic analogy: the only thing that can really guarantee that a market will function in a moral way (and not to its own destruction) is a properly oriented culture within which to operate. We need to obey those red lights even when no one else is there.

More important than that, we need to have a reasonable confidence that others are obeying the same red lights. In many ways that is the theme of Francis Fukuyama's book *Trust*, in which he noted that the countries whose markets operate best tend to have a higher degree of social trust than countries whose markets do not operate all that well. The question, naturally, is how to create this trust when you do not have it— and how to make sure that you maintain it when you do. Fukuyama puts it this way:

> If the institutions of democracy and capitalism are to work properly, they must coexist with certain premodern cultural habits that ensure their proper functioning. Law, contract, and economic rationality provide a necessary but not sufficient basis for both the stability and prosperity of post-industrial societies; they must as well be leavened with reciprocity, moral obligation, duty toward community, and trust, which are based in habit rather than rational calculation. The latter are not anachronisms in a modern society but rather the sine qua non of the latter's success.[20]

In theory we can think of many ways in which legitimate markets need to be curbed as well as all sorts of markets that we do not like, whether the market for illegal drugs or prostitution or even, in some parts of the world today, slavery. At least in the pope's eyes, the moral crime in most of these markets is the treating of humans not as beings fashioned in the image and likeness of their Creator, but as a means to someone else's end, a cog.

Now it is true that the market's drive to organize and order, when applied to something inherently wrong, can produce particularly ghastly results because the best of the market—its efficiency—is used to enhance the worst in another realm. Not only does the market trade in sin, it expands upon the sin itself by making sinning more efficient than it might otherwise be. Abortion, for example, has sadly been practiced by human beings almost since the beginning of time. But, no doubt, in John Paul's mind, while an individual abortion is one thing, an abortion industry, as exists in the United States, is quite another. The pope might call this the perversion of the market.

But here too the issue of culture is crucial, because no market will decree on abortion. It is instead a society's culture that decides whether abortion is to have the social sanction that allows it to rationalize itself into a business. There are people who would defend both the market and abortion, people who would attack both the market and abortion, and people in between who would attack one but not the other. The culture decides. At the extremes, it is true, are those market champions who view morals as entirely subjective and would resolve these moral questions "democratically." This view denies the idea that there are any external standards of right and wrong that can be applied to the market. Instead they see morality in the market as nothing more than the verdict rendered by the sum total of individual decisions.

Let us remember too that while the freedom that the market both creates and depends upon certainly enhances the opportunities for human beings to use their free will to sin, the sins themselves are by no means unique to capitalism. Prostitution, after all, has been known in all sorts of societies. So has slavery. So has greed. In socialism, where every additional person is indeed just another mouth to feed, you have precisely the Culture of Death the pope describes, in which we view others as threats to our own selves. These are all elements of the human condition that long predate capitalism. It is unromantic to say it, but poverty is brutalizing as well: see what people will do to one another when they have little of what they need to sustain themselves.

In its essence, of course, this is nothing more than the old distinction between liberty and license dressed up in different garb. In the United States, it is true, our right to the "pursuit of happiness" increasingly is pursued to its ultimate positivist conclusion: a radical autonomy that the pope rightly scored in *Evangelium Vitae*. It gets down to whether one views freedom as a radical individualism that recognizes no limits but the self or as something that itself depends on rules and limits, in much the way that we view red lights and stop signs and road rules as necessary if people are to drive.

Having experienced enough of other nations—communist, socialist, in-between—I do not believe that the sins usually charged against capitalism, such as greed and consumerism, are in fact unique to capitalism. That said, however, different economic systems have their peculiar vices, and it ought to be undeniable that a country that enshrines individual freedom is going to offer more of what we Catholics call "near occasions of sin." The more freedom and opportunities we have, the more chances we have to do as we please and not as it pleases God to have us do, one reason that Lord Acton, the nineteenth-century Catholic apostle of freedom, defined liberty as "the ability to do what one ought." In the United States, many of our hot-button issues—abortion, cloning, stem cell research, and so forth—have assumed far greater moral importance because here they come wrapped up in a market that not only helps make them possible but has a direct financial interest in doing so.

The natural impulse is to greet such abuses of freedom by seeking laws or regulations to proscribe them. And the pope could easily have given us that answer. But it is worth asking why the pope has instead looked to temper what he manifestly views as dangerous market tendencies not with laws but with culture. In the pope's mind a healthy capitalism is one that is informed by schools, church, and family, institutions in which virtue is cultivated and beliefs are forged. At times these institutions will be in tension with the larger society, especially its demands for immediate gratification.

That too is nothing new to ordinary people. Parents do that every day when their family culture clashes with something promoted in society, whether it be a ten-year-old's desire for a Britney Spears poster or a teenager's conflicting desires for premarital sexual relations, which have been glamorized by our television, film, and music industries. The newspapers are full of stories about the immense power that the market brings to such issues and the debilitating effects these market-driven influences can have.

Less often reported are the even more astounding stories of the families that are able to resist. Of the families that do resist successfully, almost all understand that they cannot rely on regulation or societal limits. They know all too well that the only way to defend their children is to inculcate in them the virtues necessary to make good choices in this world. Even in a culture as libertine as ours, not every child who is exposed to Joe Camel ends up smoking, not every child whose schoolmates are indifferent to chastity ends up sleeping around, not every child who grows up amid a music industry that denigrates women ends up beating his wife.

Market critics do not like to hear talk about the need to cultivate individual virtue. In fact, it has always struck me as interesting that, at least within the Catholic tradition, the harshest critics of the market today are also those least inclined to Catholic orthodoxy. Many of these critics often quote other encyclicals, such as *Sollicitudo Rei Socialis*, to suggest that the pope has made completely opposite statements from the ones he set out in *Centesimus Annus*. But I do not believe that the answer is to read John Paul as a schizophrenic, especially when he insists that the problem of socialism is not a problem of economics but a problem of anthropology.

I am familiar with the grim social indicators that we see everywhere in the United States, whether the rise of illegitimacy, the decline of marriage as a social norm, or the increasing coarsening of our culture. Certainly the options that the market creates help feed some of these social pathologies. But our nation's founders were not unaware of the challenge of freedom. As they well understood, there is no getting around a fundamental fact: to wit, that free societies plainly depend on virtue to survive.

That is John Paul's point too. Although he often is presented as an aging puritan at odds with modernity, his constant refrain is that man's destiny is freedom. But he reminds us that if the culture does not cultivate a proper view of that freedom—in sharp contrast to the radical autonomy that leads only to self-gratification—we shall end up destroying the virtues upon which our markets, and the affluence they create, rest.

Within this structure of markets and competition, there still remains plenty of room for redressing injustices and taking the side of the weak against the powerful. Again, as the leaders of the developing world will tell you, one of the tremendous problems they face is first world protectionism, which excludes them from our markets. The World Bank just recently released a whole report on the subject, noting, for example, that every first world job we keep through protectionism costs thirty-five jobs in the developing world.[21]

The report went on to note that traditionally we in the first world have been most protectionist in two markets that poor countries can actually compete in: textiles and agriculture. This protectionism can take many forms, and it is usually most insidious where it is not up front. Look at the opposition George W. Bush faced when he moved to let Mexican truckers on American roads.

In sum, there is much for our religiously informed activists to do even within a market society. The better economists, moreover, though they may disagree on the answers, recognize that in a science based on human activity, human nature is the critical component. It is surely no coincidence that the University of Chicago's Gary Becker specialized in what he calls "human capital." Indeed, at a Vatican conference on globalization several years back, Becker himself remarked, "I come from it at my end and you come at it from yours. But what surprises me is that we end up in the same place."

Maybe it helps to remember that when the Founding Fathers declared themselves for freedom, they minced no words: The unalienable rights of all men that they held to be self-evident were endowed not by nature but God. We are told, often enough, that the society thus created was based on rugged individualism. But as Jefferson, Madison, and Washington well knew, the freer individuals are the more they rely on their neighbors for help. This was the America that Tocqueville applauded, a nation that recognized that genuine community depends on genuine freedom.

I hope I am understood. I started with Hong Kong because Hong Kong represents one of the most open economies in the world, a place that is alive because it is free. The pope tells us repeatedly that man's destiny is freedom. An economics that understands that freedom thus will yield societies happier and healthier than the ones that see man as an animal raping the earth and breeding to his own destruction. In short, it strikes me as hard to square the demands of the Gospel with the idea of economics as a dismal science. And if that is the way we look at a process that has brought millions upon millions of people out of poverty, then our quarrel is not so much with Adam Smith or Milton Friedman as with the Providence that so clearly designed human beings to be their most prosperous at their most free.

Notes

1. Jan Morris, *Hong Kong* (New York: Viking Press, 1989), p. 72.

2. David M. Levy, *How the Dismal Science Got Its Name* (University of Michigan Press, 2001), p. 19.

3. Pope John Paul II, Laborem Exercens: *On Human Work* (Vatican City, September 14, 1981), section 9.

4. Rembert G. Weakland, "'Economic Justice for All' 10 Years Later," *America*, March 22, 1997, p. 8.

5. Second Vatican Ecumenical Council, *Pastoral Constitution on the Church in the Modern World* (Gaudium et Spes), section 39 (Vatican City: 1965), p. 1057. Quoted in *Laborem Exercens*, section 27.

6. Organisation for Economic Co-operation and Development, "Open Markets Matter: The Benefits of Trade and Investment Liberalization" (Paris: January 1999).

7. David Dollar and Aart Kraay, "Growth Is Good for the Poor" (Washington: World Bank, 2000).

8. World Bank, *The East Asian Miracle* (Oxford University Press, 1993), p. 2.

9. Pope John Paul II, Centesimus Annus: *On the Hundredth Anniversary of Rerum Novarum* (Vatican City, May 1, 1991), section 42.

10. Amintore Fanfani, *Catholicism, Protestantism, and Capitalism* (University of Notre Dame Press, 1984), p. 21.

11. Indur M. Goklany, *The Globalization of Human Well-Being*, Cato Policy Analysis 447 (Washington: Cato Institute, 2002).

12. Not least of the ironies here is that even the early communists respected the market's efficiency. As Brink Lindsey points out in *Against the Dead Hand: The Uncertain Struggle for Global Capitalism* (John Wiley & Sons, 2002), no less than Lenin once declared that "[t]he possibility of building socialism will be determined precisely by our success in combining the Soviet government and the Soviet organization of administration with modern achievements of capitalism." Which makes him one of the original third wayers.

13. Hernando de Soto, *The Mystery of Capital* (New York: Basic Books, 2000), p. 39.

14. Raymond de Roover, *San Bernardino of Siena and Sant' Antonino of Florence* (Boston: Baker Library, Harvard Graduate School of Business Administration, 1967), p. 29.

15. De Soto, *Mystery of Capital*, p. 43.

16. Pope John Paul II, *Centesimus Annus*, section 2, paragraph 13.

17. Pope John Paul II, *Laborem Exercens*, paragraph 25.2.

18. Pope John Paul II, *Centesimus Annus*, paragraph 32.

19. Ibid.

20. Francis Fukuyama, *Trust: The Social Virtues and the Creation of Prosperity* (New York: Free Press Paperback, 1996).

21. World Bank and the International Monetary Fund, "Market Access for Developing Country Exports" (Washington: September 27, 2002).

A REPLY TO McGURN

REBECCA M. BLANK

Several weeks ago an economist colleague of mine casually asked, "So, what are you working on these days?" In an unguarded moment, rather than describing one of my more typical projects, I replied, "I'm writing a series of essays on the interconnections between economics and Christian faith." The words were no more than out of my mouth than he physically backed away from me several steps, narrowed his eyes suspiciously, and demanded: "Why would you want to do that?"

Why indeed? Economics tends to be a highly secular branch of learning; economists dabble in theology at the risk of their own reputation. (This despite the fact that Adam Smith, the father of economics, was quite good at both theological and economic speculation.) And the serious study of economics is viewed with similar suspicion by many theologians.

Writing the first essay in this volume gave me an opportunity to begin to explore some of the interconnections between economic theory and core Christian beliefs. I hope that the back-and-forth dialogue between Bill McGurn and me in these follow-up essays will help us focus on some of the key issues on which we disagree. These include differences in our understanding of how and when markets function effectively, of the appropriate intersections between community (government) activity and the economy, and of the appropriate ways that individual Christians' belief and behavior overlap with economic life.

Where We Agree

In our two opening essays Bill and I agree on many things. His front-row experience observing economic change in Southeast Asia provides a useful example of the possibilities that market-oriented growth can offer. As he notes, this area of the world is not necessarily rich in resources, but it is rich in entrepreneurial energy and optimism. The result has been a series of stunning economic successes, with increases in wealth that more than accommodated growing populations. As more and more people have moved into full market participation, poverty has steadily shrunk.

I like Bill's description of the market as a series of networks. As he notes, market success depends not just on individual performance but on cooperative economic and social networks. His extended discussion of the value of capital is very useful. At least some types of possessions are not just "things"; although they may seem wasteful or prideful, they may be assets and investments that can produce a flow of services and income over time that benefit families and communities.

I am also deeply sympathetic to Bill's passionate attack on those within the church who have criticized economic discussions without having any real understanding of economics. When I have been invited to shared conversations among economists and theologians, my experience, like Bill's, has frequently suggested that the economists who participate in such conversations are more conversant with theology than are the theologians with economics. There are many reasons to disagree with the assumptions used in mainstream economic analysis to model and understand individual economic behavior or aggregate market behavior and economic growth. But to truly engage in criticism and debate, one must understand the arguments of the other side. Those within the church who ridicule or simply ignore arguments and research from within the field of economics are not engaging in real debate. And they are likely to sideline themselves from any influence on important policy debates about such issues as antipoverty efforts, foreign aid, and environmental protection.

Where We Differ

Yet the point of these responding essays is to highlight and discuss areas where we disagree. Upon reading Bill's initial essay, my immediate (and slightly amused) response was that our area of greatest difference was in the nature of the sources that we turned to for theological authority. Good Protestant that I am, I cite the biblical texts; good Catholic that he is, Bill cites the writings and encyclicals of recent popes. While I have no doubt that we could engage in a lively cross-religious discussion of the relative authority of the pope and the individual to interpret Scriptures, I fear that it would take us far afield from economic issues.

So let me turn to the economic issues on which we differ. I want to take issue with several points in Bill's initial essay, focusing on the questions of how "virtue" is encouraged in economic behavior and how the market relates to the larger social and political forces surrounding it, including its relationship to the public sector.

Bill talks a great deal in his opening essay about the networks and social connections that exist in an effective market, between and among consumers and producers all around the globe. He states that "born free, the capitalist human being is everywhere in contract to his or her neighbor." But he argues that the effective functioning of these networks relies on virtues outside the market: "[T]he market depends upon virtues—self-restraint, honesty, courage, diligence, the willingness to defer gratification—that it cannot itself create."

Bill goes on to use a traffic light metaphor for the market. The market works because most people are conditioned to following its rules in a virtuous way, rather than trying to constantly take advantage of others through personal or corporate dishonesty. Hence, even at 2:00 a.m., drivers obediently stop at a red light, not because they are likely to be caught at that particular time but because they have internalized the underlying rule that decrees that "red means stop." "The only real guarantee that a market will function in a moral way . . . is for it to have a properly oriented culture within which to operate," and, as stated later, "free societies plainly depend on virtue to survive."

Bill claims that this virtue must come from the individual and cannot be imposed by government: "[T]he nature of the market itself precludes any idea of simply regulating it into good behavior." While he is not explicit about where "good behavior" is taught, the implication is that it comes from moral teachings within the church or elsewhere that in turn shape the culture. Government, in fact, is mentioned little except to note that its regulatory role is important but should not be overused.

I do not think that it is quite that simple, nor do I believe that the cultural forces that shape markets can be so easily separated from the market itself. First, I argue that rather than developing economic institutions that rely solely upon the virtuous behavior of individuals, society should see that "virtue" is embedded within the structure of economic institutions. Second, my concern with the structure of economic institutions is heightened because economic structures are deeply embedded within political and economic structures and cannot be readily separated from them. Third, I argue that the public and private sectors are closely linked and that the public sector can have important positive effects on the economy.

What Is Virtuous Behavior within Markets?

Bill suggests that markets operate effectively when virtuous individuals bring their training to the market. He suggests, however, that virtue is taught outside the market and that when it breaks down it is not the market that is to blame but the church and other cultural institutions whose job it is to teach "right behavior." As I hope my first essay makes clear, I deeply believe in the possibilities of individual virtue, and I argue in that essay that the church should operate as a force for right behavior that teaches its members—and through their actions, the larger society—what might be meant by virtue in a market economy.

But causality does not run in a straight line from learning virtuous behavior at home to behaving virtuously in the market. Particularly in modern market economies, economic institutions are influenced by cultural and social norms and can shape our sense of what is good and acceptable. Whenever possible, virtue must be built into the institutional structures of the economy.

What do I mean by virtuous behavior in the market? Bill provides a list of individual virtues—self-restraint, honesty, courage, diligence, the willingness to defer gratification—all of which are important and help smooth market operations. But I argue that a virtuous market goes beyond individual traits. Let me suggest three additional structural traits that an effective market economy should exhibit. I explicitly refer to these as "virtuous traits"—not a term used within the context of economic analysis—because my arguments for them rely on both economic and theological reasoning.

First, *markets should function as promised in economic theory*—without market failures caused by such problems as monopolies or externalities. When markets fail—when someone acquires excess power, when adequate information is not available to consumers, or when the costs of market operation are imposed on third parties—then there is a presumption that civic action should be taken to intervene and correct such failures. When not corrected, these problems may cause higher prices; put certain producers, consumers, or workers at a disadvantage; or result in wasted resources. Much standard economic analysis is devoted to analyzing how market failures can best be detected and corrected.

Second, *markets should include and provide adequate support to as broad a number of participants as possible.* Among other things, this means that market institutions and the social institutions and legal rules that help shape market institutions should encourage employment, discourage discrimination, reward creativity and effort on the part of workers, provide the training and education that results in a productive work force, and reward companies that treat workers well and that work in partnership with the community around them. If we value community and if we are other-interested as well as self-interested, we must care about the economic opportunities available to our neighbors. A market economy will function more virtuously if it is structured to encourage and sustain broad participation.

Third, *markets and their outcomes should be used in ways that assist the most disadvantaged in society* to achieve fuller lives that are less subject to poverty and economic uncertainty. Market economies should be judged not only by the wealth that they create for individual participants, but also by the opportunities that they create for the larger community. This includes opportunities to bring more individuals into economically self-sufficient employment, as well as opportunities to reduce poverty and suffering among those who cannot work. In many cases these opportunities are created by the public and not-for-profit sectors, working together with market participants. To state it another way, a virtuous economy is one in which both the individual behavioral norms and the government and private structures that surround markets reflect the Christian mandate to care for the poor and the disadvantaged.[1]

"Virtue" in this sense requires more than individually virtuous behavior; it also requires a set of economic and government structures that ensure that attention is paid to the issues mentioned. It means that outside monitoring agencies (like the Securities and Exchange Commission, which oversees stock market transactions) should be established to make sure that the rules that guarantee economic fair play are followed and enforced. It means that certain types of temptations should be removed to prevent problems before they arise, in the same way that today's antitrust laws prevent too many mergers within an industry and lower the risk of any one company gaining excess market power. It means that rather than relying on the virtue of employers to ensure that workers are treated fairly, society should see that standards for the fair treatment of workers (including health and safety rules, fair employment practices, and pension regulations) are enacted into law.

It is important for individuals to have a collective sense of what constitutes right behavior; we all need to be taught by our parents and our community that there are virtuous forms of behavior that are expected of us by our fellow human beings. But we also need a set of economic and legal institutions that do not rely on individual virtue alone but that both encourage and enforce good behavior, assuring us that others—even those who were not well trained by their parents—are likely to follow the same rules. It may fall to the public sector in particular to create structures that monitor and sustain a virtuous market.

To return to Bill's metaphor, we need to learn that we must stop at red lights, even when a police officer is not around. If we stop only when we think we will get caught, our behavior will increase the number of accidents and harm our neighbors. But our behavior is not all that matters. We also need cars with effective signaling and braking systems. We need to place stoplights where they are needed and can be seen, and they must be maintained to function reliably. In short, we need an infrastructure that makes it easy and convenient to obey the rules as well as the individual will to obey them.

The Embeddedness of Markets

The need for direct rules and regulations within the economic system that demand, encourage, and enforce appropriate behavior within markets is further underscored by the ways in which markets are deeply embedded in the social and political systems within which they operate. Too often, the market is considered a "neutral actor" that simply reflects the world around it. The argument goes much like this: If political corruption is tolerated, then markets will be corrupt. If certain ethnic or racial groups are not considered full citizens, then the market will reflect that prejudice. These problems, however, lie outside the market itself, which merely reflects the larger social and political environment.

This argument implies that one should resist changes in the economy and in economic structures. The problems observed in the market are not really problems of the market; one must change the culture that accepts political corruption or racism. When these behaviors and attitudes change, then corruption and discrimination in the market will disappear.

This argument is not entirely wrong, but it is incomplete. Clearly economic institutions and behaviors are closely linked with and shaped by political and social institutions, but economic institutions are not just acted upon by other institutions. Economic institutions also shape social norms and political practices; they are not just mirrors of the larger society but also key actors in it.

For instance, assume that employers refuse to promote women out of low-paying, entry-level jobs. As a result, poverty among female-headed families is extremely high. It is problematic to argue that the underlying cause is social acceptance of sexist attitudes and gender inequality. In this case, the direct cause of higher poverty is discrimination embedded within the functioning of the economy. Antidiscrimination laws that force employers to offer equal economic opportunities may mitigate that poverty, and they may also help change social attitudes and norms.

The market is almost never a neutral force; it reflects the political structure and social norms of the system within which it operates. In this sense, I do not believe in "free markets." The market always operates within constraints. Proposals to regulate the market—to abolish child labor, to pay a minimum wage, to prohibit discrimination—typically reflect changing social and political norms within a society. It is absolutely appropriate to call on the government as well as other political and social institutions to ensure "virtue" in the functioning of our common life, whether in its economic, political, or social aspects. Much evidence suggests that appropriate market regulations can be effective in such areas as reducing child labor and increasing school-going among children and teens, in reducing employment discrimination, and in improving environmental and health outcomes among workers and consumers.

One way to make this argument in theological language is to return to the claim that for Christians choices are not morally neutral. Choices that pull us toward God are to be preferred to those that pull us away. The problem lies in discerning what constitutes right behavior, that is, what moves us closer to God. An immediate implication is that in our economic lives we must try to discern the economic choices that pull us toward God. If we believe that economic choices are not morally neutral, then we cannot view the market as a neutral institution. Like other choices in our lives, our economic choices—individual and collective—are opportunities to practice our Christian commitment to love and to serve others as well as ourselves.

Public-Private Links

Bill's initial essay clearly accepts the necessity of government involvement in the economy. He writes, "Government regulation and intervention may be necessary in many parts of our lives, an outcome of socially accepted efforts to keep the market away from those areas where it overreaches." But he comments that there are limits to regulation and that "whole countries are still paying" for the belief that one can regulate the market "into moral channels without losing any of its necessary dynamism." In short, Bill agrees with the necessity for regulation to combat problems of market failure and to restrict the scope of the market in certain cases. He appears, however, to be wary of using government to alter market outcomes to any great extent.

Allowing governments to regulate markets only when necessary to avoid problems of market failure—the exception typically made within economic theory—creates too narrow a scope for government. I argue at length in my initial essay that government, as well as the private not-for-profit sector, must do more. This includes limiting markets for certain products that should not be "commodified" and altering market outcomes to reflect social values other than efficiency and productivity. For instance, if the market does little to help those who are currently unable to work, the government should provide assistance, including training to help those people enter the market.

The narrower view of government—that its primary role in the economy is to correct occasional cases of market failure—is problematic for many reasons. This narrow view perpetuates the image that public and private functions are separate and opposable spheres. It is frequently argued that the private sector should operate as freely as possible without government interference, the presumption being that when the public sector acts to rein in the private sector, it makes things worse. To use the language of economics, government regulation often is assumed to create inefficiencies. This view of the public sector as the enemy of the private sector is at best a vast simplification that ignores the realities of a complex economy.

In many cases public and private functions should be viewed as cooperative. Government action often supports and expands the opportunities for the private sector. Let me provide only a few examples of this. In almost every country education has some public support at all levels, from elementary school through college. By supporting an educated work force, government expands the opportunities for productivity. The court system provides the legal structure necessary to assure private enterprise that contracts will be enforced and that fair play will prevail. Government support of transportation and communications systems creates opportunities for trade.

Nowhere is the complementarity of public and private action more apparent than in the developing world. Effective government support of a country's education, legal, health, and transportation systems is a key determinant of how promising its opportunities are for economic development. Even some government actions that restrict private sector activity—such as prohibitions on child labor or on prostitution—may in the long run enhance the opportunities for economic growth by encouraging alternative activities that promise greater productivity.

Observe, for instance, the example of Southeast Asia, which Bill returns to throughout his essay. The economic success of the region has not been due just to the operation of unfettered markets. As Bill notes, its success has occurred in part because of a set of cultural and behavioral patterns that encourage entrepreneurship. But its success also has occurred because of political structures that allow markets to flourish, with appropriate legal restrictions to prevent the accumulation and abuse of economic power; because of government incentives that encouraged local industry and made foreign investment attractive; because of subsidies that encouraged education, increasing the productive skills of the population; and because of astute diplomacy that created political connections that in turn smoothed economic connections. The resulting economic growth in Southeast Asia expanded the resources available to government to invest in additional infrastructure. The public and private sectors of these economies worked in a coordinated way, each enhancing the other.

There is no doubt that government activities can become too burdensome on an economy. Bill is right to cite evidence over the past half-century of the limits of planned economies in which market dynamics are constrained by bureaucratic rigidity. But many countries with larger public sectors than that of the United States have flourished economically. The key issue is not the size of the government but the extent to which government activities are well chosen and effectively implemented.[2] The role of government in the economy is to provide for those collective needs that cannot be met privately. In this role, the government is not the enemy but the partner of the market economy.

Summary

Bill McGurn's essay and my essay complement and agree with each other more than they disagree. In particular, we are in agreement on the most fundamental and important point, namely, that Christian faith and economic life cannot and should not be separated. We also agree that at this particular point in history the market economy is the best mechanism yet devised for managing economic affairs. Even so, it has many flaws. No one would look at our national or world economy and believe that our current mode of economic organization has come close to solving the problems of economic need, poverty, and uncertainty that face far too many of our citizens.

Both of us take these serious problems as challenges that should actively concern and engage faithful Christians, but we do not want to throw away all that we have gained because of the problems that remain. Effectively functioning markets have produced a greater level of economic security for more people than anyone would have conceived possible a few centuries ago. We need to celebrate that, even as we work to provide the structures and institutions—private, public, and church-related—that help to address ongoing economic problems.

Notes

1. It is worth noting that there are many secular arguments for designing government and private structures so that they reduce disadvantage and include those who are marginalized. Christian ethics is only one possible basis for this argument.

2. I do not want to imply that government action does not have problems. In many cases, public programs may need to use market forces to discipline the growth and effectiveness of government, by fostering competition across government jurisdictions or by encouraging private sector competition. For instance, despite dire predictions to the contrary, the U.S. postal service has maintained a market niche with clearly improved service since competition emerged from carriers like Federal Express or UPS.

A REPLY TO BLANK

WILLIAM McGURN

Rebecca blank and I were formed in quite different Christian traditions, hers originating in the German Evangelical and Reformed churches, continuing through the United Church of Christ, and culminating as a member of a Presbyterian congregation. I confess that I am not familiar with the nooks and crannies of the approach to social questions taken by these faith traditions, though the Protestant origins of the United States suggest to me that in many ways they have parts that are congenial to my own outlook—perhaps more congenial than the tradition of the Roman Catholic Church in America. (With Orestes Brownson, I would distinguish between the teaching tradition of the church and the tradition of the church as it has played out in specific places and times.) A full confession requires the admission that while I believe my own take on the market to be eminently orthodox and resonant with the teachings of Pope John Paul II in particular, mine is by no means dominant in the way the Catholic faith is taught in America today.

I will devote a little more attention to why it is significant that Rebecca and I, for all our differences, approach the issues, at least on the surface, from strikingly similar angles. What it suggests to me is not so much that we have a particular congruency of views but that the violent disagreements between promarket and antimarket Christians are not so much about Christian social principles as about the facts of economic life. That is to say that often help-the-poor schemes are put forward in ignorance of even the most basic truths of economics and that it is difficult to get across that when economists object it is as an engineer might object to a dangerously unsound structure: not on moral grounds but because it ignores the laws of gravity and therefore will collapse. This, to me, is a critical and much overlooked bone of contention. My own experience suggests that the bloodiest issue comes down to whether the market is, as I believe, a reflection of and accommodation with human nature, or whether it is, as many on the opposite side evidently believe, a fundamentally disordered enshrinement of greed.

If I were to summarize Rebecca's argument, it appears to me as follows: that the market assumes that the individual is out to maximize his or her self-interest; that the market does a good job of ensuring efficiency but that there are some things that ought not to be measured by efficiency; that the government rightly intervenes in those areas where the market either fails or is not adequate to the task; that the church's job is to remind society of all these distinctions. Up to a point we have no serious disagreement here, at least in principle. My honest guess, however, is that we should have plenty of disagreement once it came to trying to apply these broad principles to specific circumstances.

Before elaborating on the areas where I suspect we would have our differences, I would like first to show where I'm coming from. My task here is much easier than it might otherwise be, because Rebecca's economic background provides her with a commendable lack of romanticism vis-à-vis the oft-dismal performance of "earlier economic communities." If I read her correctly, the nub of her argument is that when we elevate individuals maximizing their own self-interest to the highest yardstick in every arena, conflict with Christian principles is inevitable.

My own approach is, of course, necessarily colored by the Catholicism of my birth, upbringing, and adulthood. Oft-times in reading Rebecca's essay, I had the feeling we were saying much the same thing, the difference being that Catholicism supplies my views with a distinctive language and template. Dating back to *Rerum Novarum* in the nineteenth century, these Catholic principles establish in my mind not so much definitive answers but a definitive Catholic vantage point, which I would describe as social rather than socialistic (a distinction others within the fold are not as keen to make). And in Pope John Paul II we are blessed to have a man with first-hand experience of the two totalitarianisms of our time, each of which defined human beings in largely economic or purely functional terms. In his teaching, and especially in his approach to labor, capital, and human solidarity, John Paul provides an easy compatibility with my own social understandings of the market. In fact, I find them an almost perfect fit—though I suffer the penance of finding that many of my brother and sister Catholics do not see that fit at all.

Rebecca states that she is always surprised to find how difficult it is to establish a common language on these issues. In a similar vein, I find that too often debate is muddied because we use the same terms to mean different things.

Let me start with the concept of self-interest. At the outset Rebecca lists as one of the assumptions of the market that "individuals are assumed to pursue only their own self-interest, with no concern for the well-being of any other actors in the market." In a purely economic sense, that probably is the prevailing assumption, though I should caution that there is a reason those of us on the market side of the equation almost always speak of self-interest as "self-interest *properly understood*"—in the same way that Catholics speak of a "*rightly informed* conscience" rather than just conscience itself. This is a critical qualifier, given how often we find ourselves battling concepts of self-interest wrongly understood—by both market critics who think it code for unbridled avarice and market defenders who see it as license for unbridled individualism.

I appreciate that in terms of economic constructs, it is hard to escape the idea that the individual maximizing his or her self-interest is the engine propelling the market. After all, it was no less than Adam Smith who dryly noted that it is not through the benevolence of the butcher or the baker that we expect our daily bread. In fact, however, what is more striking about the classical economists such as Smith is that they *did not* assume the profit-maximizing robot that goes almost unquestioned today. To the contrary, they assumed a market—a social construct—which by definition assumes not an individual but a community united by exchange. The flip side to Smith's remark about benevolence is that the butchers and bakers are nonetheless forced to cater to our interests to get what they want for themselves. Voila!—the invisible hand.

When the issue is approached this way, my hope is that it helps illuminate an anomaly that market critics have such a hard time with: the general civility and peace that reigns in a market economy. The portrait of laissez-faire, of course, is the dog-eat-dog society where wages are driven down and everyone is out for numero uno, all of which creates a grim race to the bottom. But if you take actual market economies, life is quite the opposite.

I like to take Hong Kong, both because it was my home for nearly a decade and because it is generally acknowledged, by friends and foes alike, to be probably the closest thing we have to a pure market economy—which, like the frictionless surfaces of high school physics texts, does not exist. Certainly Hong Kong is a driven society in which extremes of wealth and poverty exist side by side. But to anyone who has lived there the dog-eat-dog characterization is a caricature. To the contrary, Hong Kong has a thriving social sector with numerous charities and private agencies working to alleviate human suffering not only in Hong Kong but throughout China as well.

Plainly the kind of society Hong Kong represents is not the Sermon on the Mount incarnate. But it is not so far removed as people might think. A frequent mistake in the social arena is to apply personal virtues to social contexts. To put it another way, our social virtues may complement our personal virtues (and I believe ultimately depend on them), but they are not the same. Not least of the weaknesses in so-called "Christian" prescriptions for economic life is the idea that the gospels are somehow a policy platform, as though the Golden Rule can be simply legislated.

The problem with this approach ought to be obvious. If people do not willingly, say, give up a percentage of their income to some cause deemed worthy, the only way to achieve the desired outcome is by force—hardly the premier Christian virtue. In sharp contrast, the market does not rely on force, not, at least, on direct force. To invoke another Catholic phrase, I would like to suggest that it promotes habit-forming virtue. That is to say, in societies where we are compelled to be attuned to our neighbors' wants and desires if we hope to sell to or contract with them, the market is inherently other-regarding. Again, to be clear, this is not the love of neighbor demanded of us. It is, rather, to acknowledge the broad incentive powers of the market, attested to by no less than Marx in his almost lyrical riff on how the bourgeoisie class compels all others to imitate it.

Much the same dynamic might be observed of whole countries. My experience is that if you're after a dog-eat-dog ethos, there's nothing like a communist society to provide it. In Hong Kong, for example, people joke about how greedy and graspy their cousins on the mainland are. I have to wonder whether this is not because in societies that do not produce wealth, a person really is pitted against his neighbor for a smaller share of a fixed pie. All of which is a long way of explaining why societies apparently based on "greed" do better and are more peaceful than societies ostensibly based on some higher ideal—such as "From each according to his ability, to each according to his needs."

So much for self-interest. Now let's speak of market limits. Even assuming that the market is not as selfish as is often presented—even assuming that it may be as altruistic as its incentives for certain behavior make it—there still remain things, as Rebecca points out, that the market does not do well primarily because it is not designed to do them at all. Inasmuch as I am not a libertarian, I would again agree with Rebecca that there are just some things that require measures that differ from those a free market provides.

Mostly these things involve human relationships. The *Wall Street Journal* editorial page has for years run a cartoon called "Pepper and Salt." I remember one a while back featuring a family at the dinner table, with the three children solemnly listening to their father. The caption? "Times are not good. I'm afraid we're going to have to let one of you go."

The punch line is a punch line precisely because of the absurdity inherent in applying the bottom line to a family bond. Though there does exist a segment of market thought that believes itself to be completely value free and concerned only with the freedom to exchange or not to exchange, that has never been more than a minority opinion. As Rebecca points out, Christians at least cannot view all choices as "morally neutral." The real question has always been, where do we draw the line?

In theory we can talk about market failure and the need for government to intervene on behalf of, say, some group with a clear need. But there are two tricky issues here. The first is the law of unintended consequences: as easy as it is to talk about government intervention to remedy market failure or to provide for a good undervalued by the business economy, in practice it is exceptionally difficult because the intervention itself can distort the market. One reason President Bill Clinton signed welfare reform into law is that something that started out as a noble effort to help the poor ultimately had created a government network ensuring only life-time dependency and family breakdown. We might say the same of urban education today, when two-thirds of Hispanic and African American children are effectively being written out of the American Dream by fourth grade (a key juncture) by a public school system that is just not ful-filling its mandate.

Rebecca says that "at best" the market ignores the poor, whereas Christianity brings them front and center. That may be true, in the literal sense that the market does not designate people "poor" or give them help. Then again, the market is not about recognizing groups. It is about free associations. And if you're like me, you note that perhaps one of the greatest differences between rich and poor is that the former have much more opportunity when it comes to association—to sell and to buy—than the poor. The lack of the opportunity for free association, such as the ability to sell one's labor, is the essence of a "marginalized" person.

Often people are thus marginalized because their country specifically limits them. In the third world, for example, the rich are largely free to come and go abroad, to buy from foreign markets what they need or desire (for example, machinery), and of course to sell to them. But the poor not infrequently enjoy none of those rights. In the Philippines, for example, while wealthy companies and families make deals with whom they like, the poor are severely restricted in their access to international markets. For most of them, access would come in the form of the expanded employment that would be generated by foreign companies that had been allowed to invest and set up shop in the Philippines, where such investment is severely restricted.

I am sure that the Protestant traditions have their own way of dealing with these things. The Catholic point of view, however, is nicely covered by the social virtue John Paul calls solidarity. Solidarity—the feeling that we are linked with our fellow humans—is not exactly the same as loving our neighbor as ourselves. What makes it a social virtue, however, is that it creates conditions more amenable to obeying the gospel commandment. To put it another way, free and open markets increase feelings of solidarity because they increase our interactions with and co-dependency on other beings.

How we define these relationships, in turn, probably determines how we are likely to view government intervention. In theory, again, we can all agree that where the market has failed, government intervention may be required to redress the situation. In practice, however, this is always a contentious exercise. In practice it has been even more difficult to identify government failure than market failure—and there are those of us who would argue that at least some of what is called market failure is really government failure. Let me return to the law of unintended consequences. Overseas aid, to take one example, sounds fine in theory. But I recall a ground-breaking study commissioned by Alan Woods, administrator for the Agency for International Development under Ronald Reagan, that showed that despite tens of billions of dollars in foreign aid "only a handful of countries that started receiving U.S. assistance in the 1950s and the 1960s has ever graduated from dependent status."[1] To the contrary, many third world countries today labor under the staggering debt they were encouraged to take out in the 1970s and 1980s by the apostles of development assistance.

It is so not only with poor countries. It is relatively easy to show the corruption and inefficiencies that plague aid programs in Africa, Latin America, and parts of Asia, but more interesting is Saudi Arabia, which did not receive aid but had huge pots of money available for development because of its oil-generated wealth. Such were the riches produced by oil that the Saudis had, for a period of almost two decades, no financial limits on what they could do. But instead of building a competitive economy, the Saudi government used the nation's oil dollars to produce a massively inefficient, supra-welfare state where the lack of a work ethic remains a scandal and the failure to produce a dynamic economy has left the nation reliant on a commodity that, like most commodities, is on a slow downward curve in real value. The point is that money is not always the solution and may sometimes be the problem.

If money is not the solution, what is? To me the answer is capital. But not capital defined in the material sense, which the Saudis had in abundance. Rather, the answer is capital in the metaphysical sense, measured by the ability of human beings to combine their intelligence and labor to create and to interact with others as they create. Both these factors are necessary for real development. Human beings need the freedom to work—by which they become integrated with others—as well as the freedom to make the most of what they have worked at through associating with others.

This is the definition John Paul seems to have in mind in *Centesimus Annus*. Though he does not (as I do) tether the market explicitly to human nature, he does argue that the chief components of wealth today are human beings' application of their minds to earth's matter and their ability to do so not in splendid isolation but in communion with their fellows.

In our time, writes the pope, mere material ownership of things is rapidly becoming less decisive as a factor of wealth than "the possession of know-how, technology and skills. The wealth of the industrialized nations is based much more on this kind of ownership than on natural resources." As for human nature, this truth cuts to the heart of Christian social teaching, in that "today the decisive factor is increasingly the person, that is, one's knowledge, especially one's scientific knowledge, one's capacity for interrelated and compact organization, as well as one's ability to perceive the needs of others and to satisfy them."[2]

In sum, the pope is saying that the two crucial factors for development that would meet the Christian standard are the freedom to create on the individual level and the freedom to associate on the social level. And it is precisely the lack of the latter—"fair access to the international market"— that the pope identifies as the "chief problem" facing poor nations.

Rebecca echoes some of this in her own factual observation that "the worst work situations often occur in low-wage jobs that require little training of or investment in the worker and for which there are many readily available job-seekers who can be hired to replace a current worker almost immediately."

So what's a Christian to do? There are two answers. The short answer is, as we would both agree, that the defining act of a Christian in a just economic order begins with the fundamental recognition that we are more than economic beings, that our economic lives are an abstraction that in real life is grounded within a larger culture. This position constitutes the core of John Paul's approach, though the equation is frequently misunderstood as a call for some "third way" that would define a rightly ordered market as some Christian halfway house between socialism and capitalism. It is a crude view but perhaps understandable for people who do not immediately grasp the centrality of the Christian claim that puts mankind above any mere system.

Certainly we should all prefer a world where our bosses, customers, and co-workers all were people who took the gospels literally and sincerely and at all times dealt with all those in their lives as though they were dealing with Christ Himself. To paraphrase Madison, however, on this side of paradise we do well not to confuse men with angels when we construct our systems.

In other words, in a world tinged by original sin, even St. Francis could not avoid the hard decisions faced by a company that has to lay off workers or go out of business altogether. If we market proponents sometimes seem soft on specific abuses, it is because we tend to worry about the effect of well-intentioned but harmful incentives and disincentives created by interventions.

In sum, about the fundamental Christian proposition—that economics is important to but trumped by our humanity—we could not agree more. It strikes me as not a coincidence that the God who made thinking beings in His own image appears to have put us in a world in which our wealth and well-being depend not only on our own freedom but on that of our neighbors.

Notes

1. Alan Woods, *Development and the National Interest: U.S. Economic Assistance into the 21st Century* (Washington: Agency for International Development, 1989), p. 112.

2. Pope John Paul II, Centesimus Annus: *On the Hundredth Anniversary of Rerum Novarum* (Vatican City, May 1, 1991), paragraph 32.

CREATING A VIRTUOUS ECONOMY

REBECCA M. BLANK

ONE OF the enjoyable aspects of writing a series of essays like this over a period of time is that it provides an opportunity to revisit and clarify one's ideas. I have presented parts of my introductory essay in this volume to several different audiences and in each case at least part of the audience has clearly interpreted my stance as asserting that "market beliefs are inconsistent with Christian beliefs." They understand me to be arguing for a dualistic view: one can adopt either the precepts of economics or the precepts of faith. Self-interest or other-interest? Individual concerns or community concerns?

Worried that others may have received the same impression, I want to use some of my space in this final essay to argue that this is not a dualistic, either/or choice. I then return to Bill's arguments for the market, focusing particularly on his responding essay, and reiterate and expand on some of our areas of disagreement.

Market Views and Faith Views: A Matter of Balance

No Christian should find it strange to balance multiple realities. We are called to both live and act in this world but not to be of this world. We are called to live with the reality of our sinfulness, but also with the reality of grace and redemption. In response to a question about paying taxes, Jesus responds, "Give to the emperor the things that are the emperor's and to God the things that are God's" (Matthew 22:21; Mark 12:17; Luke 20:25).

Our interaction with a market economy must have the same balance. A market economy is a force that can drive development, decrease poverty, encourage productivity, and reward entrepreneurial energy. But human beings have created the market, and it, like us, has many limitations. It can serve to foster greed; dehumanize individual workers; ignore the needs of the unemployed, disabled, or elderly; and lead some people to use their economic power in ways that harm their neighbors as well as the natural environment.

Nor is this a simple dualism. Outcomes are not *either* good or bad; more frequently, they are *both* good and bad. Markets can enrich the lives of some who were previously poor while excluding others; markets also can generate new jobs and encourage the development of new human talents, even while they displace or disempower others whose skills are no longer as useful.

In these multiple and contrasting possibilities, the market economy is no different than any other human institution. It is wrong to believe that persons in corporate life are more prone to lie or to misuse their power. The world of business can be a place of sinfulness and abusive behavior, but so can not-for-profit organizations, public sector agencies, or the church itself—as reflected, for example, in the recent scandals over priests who abused their power over children. All of these places can also be locations of grace, where individuals experience redemption by discovering new opportunities, where their talents are fostered and their abilities affirmed.

As I try to say in my initial essay, there is nothing wrong with self-interest or individualistic behavior, as emphasized by economic models of behavior. In many situations, this type of behavior is appropriate and even necessary. Individuals who have no sense of themselves as separate and worthwhile persons are not fully functioning human beings—yet neither are individuals who are only self-interested and who see the rest of the world as no more than a collection of individuals each pursuing his or her self-interest. It is our faith that reminds us of the possibilities of being other-interested as well as self-interested; of caring for community as well as caring for self. For those of us who live in this world, the call is to be "both/and," not "either/or." We must understand how to *balance* these demands.

The market economy particularly calls forth certain aspects of our human nature. On the positive side, it rewards us for effort; it repays our talents and encourages us to increase them through education and experience; and it provides ways to use wealth so that it creates other wealth and hence greater future possibilities. On the negative side, it can foster changes that create unemployment and impoverish hard-working people whose only flaw is being in the wrong place at the wrong time when the factories close or customer demand changes. It can encourage greed and tempt employers to treat their employees as interchangeable parts in the production process rather than as fellow human beings.

Our faith does not call us to turn our back on the market economy and on the good—or the bad—that it can do, but it does remind us that our talents are not entirely of our own making. Faith reminds us that we should not overvalue the things of this world or turn toward greed, but use our economic capacity in ways that serve God and serve our neighbors as well as ourselves. Faith reminds us that wealth is not an end in and of itself but a means to improve the well-being of ourselves and our neigh bors. Wealth can generate jobs and income and lessen poverty; it also can be used to provide valued goods to the community, such as better schools and more parks.

There is no need to make an either/or choice between participating in the market economy and being a Christian. Rather the challenge is to live in the market but not be wholly possessed by the market. Different people will find the most appropriate balance at different places along this spectrum. Those of us—most of us—who find ourselves daily in the midst of the world of commerce and consumerism must find ways to acknowledge and make use of the many good things that market economies can achieve while also organizing and nourishing our communities to treat human beings as more than economic beings.

We Need More Than Markets to Organize Economic Life

Because market economies—and the human beings who live and work inside them—have some predictable weaknesses, it is not wise to rely solely on markets to organize our economic life together. Hence the role for community-based organizations to advocate for and respond to specific individual and community needs that the market might not respond to. Organizations like the YMCA or Big Brothers/Big Sisters can provide special services to children or youth that their parents cannot afford. Churches and other local community groups provide networks of connections and assistance that people may not find among other friends or even within their own family. Such voluntary and not-for-profit organizations can play an important role in helping individuals in ways that the market economy will not.

Similarly, the government plays an important role mediating the effects of the market economy. I discussed various roles for government in my opening essay. One role of government is to ensure that the market economy functions effectively, enforcing rules about information disclosure, honest advertising, and fair treatment of customers and workers. Governments enforce such regulations not to thwart the market economy but to ensure that it operates as promised—with full information, open and fair competition, and no exclusion or discrimination.

Another role of government is to provide an alternative institutional structure in those areas where the market economy does not operate effectively. Hence we call upon the government to support parks, ensure adequate education for poor children, provide assistance to the poor and disabled, and provide for our national defense.

Finally, we use the power of government to broadly enforce certain community values that may not otherwise prevail in the market. Through the government, we limit child labor and prostitution and enforce environmental or health standards. We require workers and employers to contribute to unemployment insurance and to Social Security to support retired or disabled workers. The government is one aspect of our larger community life, and it is particularly important as a partner of the private sector and the economy. In some cases, it should act to support and encourage private transactions; in other cases, it validly acts to limit the reach of the market or to accomplish things that the market cannot do by itself.

Responding to Bill McGurn's Essays

Let me reaffirm, as Bill does on numerous occasions, that we are in agreement about many things. We both agree that the market encourages many good forms of behavior and that market growth and development has been a force for positive change in the lives of people around the world. The market has, of course, also at times functioned in ways that encouraged inappropriate behavior and harmful change, but that is not an inevitable result of markets. We both agree that there is a role for government in regulating certain types of market behavior and in engaging in modest forms of redistribution of wealth. But Bill has more trust in the ability of markets operating on their own to produce effective outcomes for most participants. As a corollary to this, he argues for a more limited role for government than I do.

In this section I respond to three particular aspects of Bill's argument with which I take issue. I discuss his claim that markets create civility and peace; his separation of family life from economic life, as an entirely different realm; and his argument that government frequently is ineffective and that its actions often do more harm than good.

MARKETS: A SOURCE OF CIVILITY AND PEACE?

In his responding essay, Bill talks about "the general civility and peace that reigns in a market economy"; indeed, he claims that markets need those conditions to function well. Cooperation is mandatory for the free exchange of labor and goods, hence the market encourages cooperation. One implication is that the need for market intervention by government or by community-based groups is limited. The market itself will resolve many problems.

Effective and functioning markets do rely upon a high degree of communication and trust. But such trust need not reside in another individual, but in the clear enforcement of legal and behavioral expectations about appropriate market behavior. I need not individually like—nor even know much about—the people who buy my product. But I do need to know that they can be expected to pay the agreed-upon price at the agreed-upon time. Similarly, I need not know anything about those who make a product that I buy, but I have to be able to trust the production and delivery system to provide a product that is what it claims to be and to trust the legal system to enforce sanctions if it is not.

I need to believe that others are willing to operate by the same economic rules that I do. When I do not trust an impersonal system, then I might seek out products whose provenance is known to me. For instance, if I really care about buying fruit that has never been sprayed with insecticide, then I might be more willing to buy from the nearby farmer whose practices are known to me than from a grocery store bin labeled "pesticide free."

Bill's argument that markets particularly promote civility and cooperation because they require it for effective operation is an interesting one, but one for which I think the evidence is quite mixed. I agree that there are indeed ways that markets promote cooperation. Especially if I expect to establish a long-term customer or employee relationship, I have an incentive to treat other individuals with respect and fairness. I want them to keep doing business with me for a long time to come; hence I might be concerned about my reputation for quality work and fair treatment.

I can think of a number of situations in which these incentives for cooperation and civility break down, however—situations in which markets may *not* lead to cooperation and civility. First, the market provides monetary rewards; for those with a predeliction toward greed it can provide incentives and opportunities for abusive economic behavior. This may be particularly true with short-term or one-time economic interactions. For instance, there are many anecdotes of individuals being overcharged or shoddily served when stopping at a gas station off an interstate highway. The gas station owner knows that individuals who live out of state probably will never be back again; if they are in need of immediate car repairs, that gives the station owner an opportunity to abuse the power that he or she has in owning the only convenient service station.

Abuse of economic power can occur on a broader scale as well. Markets reward the acquisition of wealth and encourage those with wealth to try to consolidate their economic power. More economic power means more control of prices as well as more control of the terms and conditions of employment. Of course, the market continually fights the accumulation of power by encouraging competitors who will sell at a lower price or pay higher wages to good workers. But in many cases competition does not work well enough to prevent one producer, for at least a short period of time, from gaining excess market power, which it can misuse.

One result is a regular succession of business scandals. Enron grew into a market giant and for some period of time was able to hide information about its shaky finances. When its shady business practices finally came to light in 2002, it collapsed, leaving its workers unemployed and its shareholders with worthless stock. In a similar way, in the mid-1980s savings and loan institutions took advantage of legal loopholes to engage in extremely risky investment behavior. When what was happening finally became clear, a whole industry collapsed, sending ripple effects throughout the economy. These are only the most visible, public scandals; there is a steady stream of news reports detailing efforts by various companies to defraud customers, bribe inspectors, misrepresent their finances, or hide crucial information from employees.

Most businesses do not engage in that sort of behavior. But such scandals happen often enough to create a level of ongoing distrust in the media and the public mind of business, and especially of "big business." The important point is that these scandals are not just "something that happens" because of a few bad apples. Yes, they typically involve individuals in leadership positions who lack a strong moral compass. But they also are the direct result of a market economy that consistently sends the message that more sales, higher profits, and higher growth rates define economic "success." While none of these things inherently lead to fraudulent behavior, the market system surely encourages a mind-set that can lead to fraudulent behavior on the part of those arrogant enough to push the rules a bit too far when they find themselves with economic power.

A second way that markets can break down civility and trust is through the economic pain associated with the normal functioning of market economies. A market that encourages innovation and creativity will invent new technologies that in turn supplant older technologies. Blacksmiths give way to auto mechanics. Stenographers give way to voice-recognition software. Machine operators give way to robotic machinery. Reference librarians give way to computer search engines. These new processes may help produce better products or more efficient services, but they also lead to worker displacement and disemployment. Even when the new technologies create as many or more jobs than they displace, they often require skills that the displaced workers do not have.

I understand the value of economic and technological change, and I believe that in many cases it leads to better outcomes for many people. But change is almost never costless. Market processes, even when they benefit large numbers of people, can be extremely cruel to those individuals whose skills have become obsolete or whose jobs have moved elsewhere. Economic growth and market expansion have an ugly underside that should not be ignored, especially by those who emphasize the benefits of the market.

Just as corporate scandals create an underlying distrust of business, so also the regular experience of unemployment, displacement, and economic loss creates an underlying distrust of the market. Most people in market economies have either experienced these problems directly or can tell stories of parents, children, or friends who have faced serious economic hardship not because they did something wrong but because of larger market trends and cycles that led firms to fire workers or relocate jobs.

None of these examples lead me to retract my statements in earlier essays about the many benefits that the market can offer. But they make me wary of agreeing that markets primarily promote civility and cooperation. Some aspects of the market clearly do reward and encourage cooperation. But other aspects of the market can be socially disruptive and can foster public distrust and anger. We are back to where we started in this essay: the market is neither wholly good nor wholly bad. Markets can be beneficial, but even when functioning effectively they entail real social costs. Other institutions within a market economy—families and community and government organizations—must act at times to buffer and protect individuals from the problems that a market economy creates.

THE SPHERE OF THE MARKET

Bill argues that the market exists as one part of our community life. He uses a recent *Wall Street Journal* cartoon to illustrate that family life exists in a separate sphere and operates by a different set of rules. Individuals come into the market from their particular family and cultural background, and the market must rely on the values and ethical standards that individuals have acquired outside the market and bring to it. In this sense, the market is embedded within a culture and the religious teachings of that culture. Hence individuals come to the market as ethically trained persons, or they do not. It is the responsibility of the church, of families, and, perhaps to a lesser extent, of public institutions to train individuals in the appropriate interpersonal ethical behavior that helps "grease the wheels" of the market.

Let me respond first by noting that I find the separate spheres claim troubling. I think our lives are much messier and that the different aspects of our life together spill over and intermingle in such a way that often the notion of separate spheres is not really useful. On one hand, in my initial essay I discussed the many ways in which "marketized thinking" has invaded many areas outside economics. We apply cost-benefit tests to marriage decisions and think about the opportunity costs before volunteering for a church committee. Economic language and economic models are used far outside the economic sphere of life.

On the other hand, I also argue in my initial essay that some of the same principles that apply to family life should also be present in at least some ways in our economic lives: There are times in the market when other-interest should exist beside self-interest; there are times when concern for the community should preempt concern for the individual. These alternative values may be *more* present in family life than in economic life, but they need to be at least somewhat present in both. These are less different spheres than overlapping spheres. A continuum of values and perspectives is present in both the market and family life, but they have different weights and saliency in one area than in another.

Putting aside concerns with the separate spheres argument, let me more broadly argue with the claim that individual ethics ensure a well-functioning market. I believe that individual ethics are a necessary attribute for market participants in an effectively functioning market, but individual ethics by themselves are not fully sufficient.

We cannot rely on all individuals to be ethical, or—even more problematic—to define ethical behavior in the same way. In a more diverse and heterogeneous society such as that of the United States, it is difficult to identify a universally acceptable culture or set of ethical constructs. In times past, it was perhaps assumed that the church would provide a foundation of broadly accepted teachings to guide individuals' public behavior, but that is no longer a safe assumption in a country where religious diversity is growing, along with the number of those who do not identify themselves with any religion. We can bewail or praise this lack of a common religious culture; certainly it creates a variety of social challenges far beyond the functioning of markets. Increasingly, our ethical standards are defined by secular principles—by self-help books like *The Seven Habits of Highly-Effective People* and *All I Really Need to Know I Learned in Kindergarten*—rather than by Sunday School lessons.[1]

Please note that I do not argue that religious diversity means the diminishing of individual ethical standards. I merely argue that it lessens the number of common ethical and religious references and touchstones that we can use publicly or that we can expect a wide share of the population to recognize. That makes it increasingly difficult to claim that the market can rely on common cultural assumptions and restraints on behavior.

I believe that in a diverse cultural environment and with a market that produces both opportunities and problems, three economic and social attributes must be present for the market to function effectively—that is, for the good attributes and effects of the market to predominate, while some of its more problematic effects are minimized.

First, a society is needed in which individuals pay attention to basic virtues in their social life together. Individuals need to be motivated by their own internal distaste for socially undesirable behavior—they have to believe that lying and cheating is a bad idea—since most of the time individuals are not restrained by anything other than their individual moral sense of right and wrong. Any functioning society requires individuals to be schooled in how to live cooperatively and treat other people humanely; that is true for both its economy and other civic spheres. These individual notions of appropriate behavior can be based on religious beliefs or on more secular ethical principles.

Second, economic systems should be set up to provide appropriate incentives for good behavior. If at all possible, an economy should be organized around the proposition that cheaters never prosper. This requires a legal system that clearly defines what is or is not approved behavior and imposes clear sanctions on unethical market behavior. This requires that those who do misrepresent or defraud in their business practices face clear punishments. This requires positive rewards for good behavior. Companies that are known to treat their workers well should be able to hire better workers. Workers who work harder and better should receive higher wages.

The market typically functions to reward productivity, hence providing these incentives without any external intervention. Market economists regularly make the claim that more productive workers and better-managed firms should reap greater economic rewards. Many argue that this allows the market to "do well by doing good"—that is, that firms that are more economically successful can in turn pay higher wages to their workers while providing higher-quality services to their customers.

I am not convinced by the argument that the market alone will create the incentives and rewards that foster this behavior. It is true that more productive firms often reap economic rewards and can use those rewards to benefit their workers and customers. But other firms might succeed because they are able to hire lower-wage labor or provide very low-quality goods to lower-income families who cannot afford anything better. In short, there are many ways to increase profits; greater productivity is one route, but cutting costs or quality is another, and consumers may be unable to detect the difference at the point of purchase.

In addition, nothing guarantees that market rewards will be distributed fairly to all who participate. Employers who do well may or may not reward their workers. In fact, they may believe that their higher profits occurred because they paid lower wages to their workers, or they may use their profits to reward top management, without raising the salaries of any mid-level or lower-level employees.

Third, because the market system itself will not always establish the appropriate incentives, I believe that there must be non-market-based structures—public agencies, government-supported programs, and voluntary community associations like churches or not-for-profit organizations—that supplement, restrain, and at times overturn the results of the market in response to other social values and priorities. In all fairness, I note that Bill clearly supports such structures and organizations as well. I see them—especially government agencies—occupying a more important role and having a larger scope, however.

I stated various roles for government in my first essay and repeated them earlier in this one. The government offers a way to construct organizations and programs that respond to common needs and desires that the market itself does not respond to. In a similar way, our churches and other community-based organizations also supplement the market economy and, when necessary, protect us from it. These organizations do other things as well, many of them entirely unrelated to economic life. But at least one of their organizational purposes is to provide assistance to families to help them cope with the problems and the possibilities of a market economy.

An effective market economy needs all of these things: individuals must have a strong sense of appropriate behavior; market institutions need to function competitively, providing clear rewards for functioning well and punishment for misinformation, fraudulent behavior, or misuse of economic power; and public and private institutions need to supplement the market, redistributing resources to help people who are excluded or marginalized by the market and working with the market to ensure that important public values—which may or may not be valued by the market—are supported and promoted, such as health or environmental standards.

DEALING WITH GOVERNMENT FAILURE

Bill is skeptical of the ability of government to improve on market outcomes. A major concern raised in his responding essay is the problem of "government failure." As he notes, it is difficult to get government incentives right in setting policy. He cites a number of examples of government failure in which corruption or misinformation has resulted in ineffective and even destructive public policies, such as the failure of overseas aid to promote economic development. As Bill notes, you cannot legislate the Golden Rule, and it is messy and difficult to try. One can end up doing more harm than good by trying to create a superstructure of government agencies and programs aimed at remedying specific problems in the market economy.

Certainly there are plenty of examples of ineffective government efforts, many of them well-meaning. Bill mentions the failure of U.S. foreign aid to stimulate economic development. Because it is distributed largely on the basis of political objectives, it is perhaps unsurprising that typically it is not very effective in assisting economic development in the poorest nations. Another example is the federal government's effort to stimulate urban renewal and provide housing assistance, which resulted in the construction of segregated, high-crime, and socially isolated high-rise public housing projects in our inner cities.

I also share Bill's concern about relying on government solutions in many situations in which the market can function more effectively. The last fifty years provide clear economic lessons about the negative effects when government intervention is too extensive. Nations that have tried to implement centrally planned economies have faced serious problems with economic stagnation, low productivity, inefficiency, and wasted resources.

But I teach at a school of public policy because I believe deeply in our ability to run a host of effective government-based programs and agencies. In fact, schools of public policy are designed to try to teach students how to avoid the worst problems of government inefficiency and bureaucracy and make government work effectively. Let me summarize a few of the lessons that I think are important.

Most government agencies have a very difficult job—much more difficult than that of private sector companies. Within the private sector, the goals often are quite clear—for example, "Set up an organization that makes a product people want at a price they can afford." The goals facing government agencies often are much less clear. On one hand, they are commissioned to provide some sort of public service—maintain the roads, provide education, or monitor wastewater emissions. On the other hand, because they are public agencies, other agendas often are imposed upon them. Their leadership is often appointed or elected by groups or individuals who are not themselves highly informed about the agency. Often they are caught in the midst of political battles and their budgets are punished or rewarded for reasons that have little relation to their overall mission. When administrations change, agencies may be entirely restructured or redirected, losing momentum and expertise. Some government programs are required to serve literally millions of people every month, through systems that must be able to adapt to thousands of variations in client background. We demand absolute accuracy from the tax, Social Security, and postal systems, which operate on a scale far greater than that of most private sector companies. I believe that only rarely is the right question "Why can't the government do more?" Much more often, it should be "How does the government accomplish so much, given all of the problems that it faces?"

Despite those problems, many committed and competent people work for and direct public agencies. One of the privileges of my life has been the opportunity to become acquainted with a number of long-term civil servants who work on human service issues within state and federal governments. Their level of knowledge is impressive, and their commitment to their job often exceeds that of many private sector workers. They chose this work—despite its headaches and lack of major financial rewards—because they think that it is good work that it is important to do.

The services that government agencies are asked to provide often are complex. Monitoring pollution in an effective way requires constantly updating technical expertise and applying it to a wide variety of regional locations, with real-time monitoring. One part of the agency must be ready to battle recalcitrant companies in court, while another part of the agency must try to work cooperatively to reduce the legal battles. Similarly, running effective welfare-to-work programs requires a mix of skills. Welfare recipients who can move into work (with some assistance) need to be distinguished from those who are not "work-ready" because of their family or personal circumstances. One part of the agency needs to work with the welfare recipients to help them prepare for work; another part needs to work in the private sector to identify likely employers. Caseworkers need to be "job coaches," but they also need to be conversant with all the other services and programs (such as food stamps, child care subsidies, or public health insurance) that their clients may need to survive economically in a low-wage job. People who run these welfare offices need to be extremely competent managers who can organize a multitask environment to serve a highly heterogeneous population.

When government programs run into difficulties, often it is for specific reasons. Let me list a few. First, government agencies can be too caught up in politics to pay adequate attention to their service mission. Programs can be seriously hurt by too-frequent leadership changes or reorganizations that destroy the sense of mission and fail to use the acquired knowledge of workers. Second, government programs can lose their effectiveness when there is a broader pattern of corruption or patronage within government. While certainly not unknown in the United States, it is an even greater problem in many developing countries, where corruption and bribery are common. Third, government programs often are created without adequate funding. They are asked to take on complex tasks with nonfunctional computers, too few staff, and inadequate enforcement powers. When public welfare programs in our inner cities are so underfunded that they must hire low-skilled workers to handle 500 or more cases at one time, it is no surprise that welfare programs are the target of complaints by recipients and taxpayers alike. Fourth, government programs can be caught in rigid bureaucratic systems that limit their flexibility to promote or hire good workers or that allow procedural requirements to take precedence over common sense.

None of this is unique to government. Indeed, problems of corruption, bureaucracy, and an unclear mission can bedevil the private sector as well. In organizing the institutional structure of government, some changes can improve public sector performance. Agencies should be given enough independence so that they are at least somewhat protected from short-term political battles and mood swings; that often requires limiting patronage and the number of political appointees in senior management jobs. State and federal personnel systems should be flexible enough to adapt to different environments and different work needs; they also should strictly enforce anticorruption standards within both the public and private sector to establish a social norm of noncorrupt decisionmaking. And attracting and retaining good people for government positions at all levels must be a priority. That means paying competitive wages and providing a public budget to support the agency at a reasonable level.

Let me emphasize two important points about government agencies and government programs. First, many of them do quite a good job of providing exactly the service they are meant to provide, often in the face of a complex and occasionally hostile environment. There is clear evidence that hunger in the United States has declined because of the food stamp program and that public health insurance programs have improved health care for children. There is clear evidence that poverty among the elderly has fallen because of the Social Security system and that pollution has been reduced by the enforcement of clean air and clean water standards. There is clear evidence that the police and courts often make the right decisions and that public schools help prepare many children for literate adulthood. Roads are maintained and construction codes enforced to reduce fires and make public spaces accessible to the disabled. Millions of people benefit from parks and public recreation facilities every day, and millions of letters are accurately delivered by the U.S. Postal Service.

Second, despite all of the problems that many government agencies face, often there is no better alternative than to work on reorganizing and improving services within those agencies. A colleague of mine used to say, "The only thing worse than a market economy is a nonmarket economy." Similarly, I would claim that "the only thing worse than the government provision of many services is the absence of government provision of those services." Few of the major services provided by government can be easily organized through private markets. Indeed, the reason the government was organized to provide these services is that market failure prevents them from being effectively provided by the private sector or because they are designed to monitor and enforce certain restrictions on the private sector.

Running a government effectively requires skill and resources. Government systems are never costless, and they always can be improved. Like market economic systems, the government provision of goods and services creates certain advantages and certain problems. Just as I believe that the market should be allowed to operate as openly as possible when market competition is strong and markets function effectively, so I believe that the government should be given the resources and support to operate as effectively as possible to implement programs that reflect collective social values and that are ineffectively provided in market economies.

At the risk of repeating myself one more time, the question is again one of balance. Overreliance on the market is as dangerous as overreliance on an overly large and powerful government. Good public and private leaders understand that the public and private sectors are partners, each operating in areas where it is most effective and most needed.

A Final Word

This series of essays has given me a chance to think in a more sustained way about the interactions between economic needs and public concerns and about the ways in which Christian faith might shape one's view of market economics and the public and private sector institutions that support our economic life together. I hope that I have made a few fundamental points in my essays.

First, markets frequently are a source of economic opportunity and hope. The development and expansion of modern economic markets has allowed large numbers of people to escape poverty. But markets often do not function as effectively in practice as in theory. Some individuals and organizations acquire economic power that allows them to restrict competition, hide information about their products, or mistreat their workers. Some market institutions are embedded in systems where corruption or discrimination abound, leading to the exclusion and impoverishment of those who are not allowed to fully participate in the economy. Those in the church who wish to improve the economic lives of their neighbors around the globe should both encourage and support the expansion of effective markets, while working to put in place legal and government structures designed to push markets to operate competitively.

Second, we in the church are called to live in the modern economy, but to maintain values that may sometimes conflict with those of the market. We need to balance self-interest with other-interest and find ways to exercise other-interest not just among our families and friends but among our co-workers and in our economic transactions. We need to think about community interests as well as individual interests, at times opting for government structures that enforce community priorities that the market may not value, such as job safety, environmental protection, or redistribution programs that provide resources for those who cannot achieve economic self-sufficiency in the market.

Third, the government plays an important role in helping markets function more effectively by ensuring a common legal framework, full disclosure of information, and anticorruption laws. But the government also is important in establishing common values and priorities. This is particularly important in religiously and culturally diverse countries, in which one cannot assume that all citizens operate within a common ethical and religious framework. For a Christian individual, the government provides mechanisms that reach out to neighbors throughout the globe.

Government-based outreach programs can operate more broadly than individually organized efforts and often work in cooperation with church-based or not-for-profit community-based programs.

Except for those few among us who elect to withdraw into monastic life, most Christians in the United States must live in a world where the market economy is a dominant and vital institution. Our economic lives are not separate from our Christian lives. Like all other aspects of who we are as humans, our economic choices and behaviors are subject to the judgment of God and are open to God's grace and revealing presence. We are both economic and spiritual creatures.

I have found this dialogue deeply challenging and enlightening. It has forced me to think more clearly about how our economic lives interweave with our faith-based commitments. I hope that these essays might generate continued discussion of this issue among many people and at many levels within and outside the Christian church.

Notes

1. Stephen R. Covey, *The Seven Habits of Highly Effective People: Restoring the Character Ethic* (Simon and Schuster, 1989); Robert Fulghum, *All I Really Need to Know I Learned in Kindergarten: Uncommon Thoughts on Common Things* (New York: Villard Books, 1988).

CREATIVE VIRTUES OF THE ECONOMY

WILLIAM McGURN

WE DISAGREE after all. And in more than degree.

In essence Rebecca's argument has two prongs. The first is that for markets to work the way Christians would find desirable—honestly, fairly, bringing wealth and opportunity to the least of our brothers—requires a social capital that must be more than the mere aggregate of the virtues of the individual players who make up that market. Rebecca's second contention is that government has much to contribute to this right ordering of markets—and that I am more skeptical than she is here. I agree wholeheartedly with the first. And I plead guilty to the second.

Before I go down that path, however, let me take up a perceptive observation that Rebecca makes about our differing approaches: hers leaning more to Scripture, mine more to papal encyclicals. There is more than irony at work here. Without wishing to lend my own imprimatur to the Max Weber version of history, surely it is fair to say that my Roman Catholic co-religionists have, at least in recent history, approached the market with more trepidation than many of those in the Protestant traditions, owing in part, I believe, to a pronounced Catholic discomfort with even honest wealth that strikes me as absent from at least the American varieties of Protestantism and Judaism. My reference to encyclicals consequently reflects the bulk of my experience, which has been devoted to trying to demonstrate the congruity of markets with Roman Catholic social teaching.

There is another, more positive reason. Not least of the attractions of Catholic social teaching is that it provides a ready language and structure. Pope John Paul II, with his first-hand experience of the twin totalitarianisms of the age and his grappling with the contours of a just economic arrangement, has added powerfully to the vocabulary by which we morally comprehend market interactions. Probably this would be worth a discussion on its own.

But not here. The market does indeed require social virtues—a social framework that is indeed more than the sum of the individuals that participate in it. That is to say, Rebecca and I agree that the kind of market that we believe Christians must strive for requires social virtues and incentives of its own to function rightly. Our disagreement over the role of government, however, reflects not simply a difference in how much government regulation we believe to be necessary for the job but—and this is often overlooked in such discussions—our more fundamental divide over how we define the problem that government is supposed to fix.

I am no libertarian. Which is only to say that, in acknowledging that the market requires, encourages, and rewards certain virtues, I do not believe that these required virtues are either sufficient or self-sustaining. That leaves only two other potential checks on the market. The first is politics, or government. The second is culture, whose most obvious component is religion. If I had to sum up our respective propositions, I would say that Rebecca would probably consider it naïve to think of culture as strong enough to counter powerful market forces while I deem it even more naïve to expect government, which enjoys a monopoly of force, to do it properly. On paper that might sound like a difference solely in degree, but if I'm right it would mean that in practice, as specific problems arise, Rebecca would be looking largely to government for solutions and I to culture. And I think that that is precisely what does happen in the specific instances that she and I cite.

Critics tend to read this as a blind faith in markets. And the debate over the inefficiency of state regulation is an old and tired one. That does not change the fact that there is ample good reason to entertain strong doubts about government when it moves beyond the setting of ground rules that apply to everyone (enforcement of contracts and so forth) to intervening to effect specific outcomes. To illustrate what I mean, let me move from theory to the specific instances that Rebecca herself brings up, areas where we probably would agree on the desired ends but would strongly disagree on means. She mentions three—eliminating child labor, ensuring a minimum wage, and reducing discrimination—as though they self-evidently prove the case for corrective government intervention.

But let me take on these same examples from a somewhat different perspective. Let's start with what is probably the most repugnant: child labor. I appreciate that in an affluent nation such as the United States the very notion that children could be put to work can be nearly incomprehensible. That, rest assured, is not the way it looks from the dinner tables and government chanceries of the third world. I say this as someone who served as senior editor for the *Far Eastern Economic Review*, a magazine that once ran a cover featuring a twelve-year-old Bangladeshi factory worker under the heading "Child Labour: It Isn't Black and White."[1]

Let me illustrate the theme of that story. Back in 1992, Wal-Mart CEO David Glass was ambushed by an NBC TV *Dateline* reporter who showed video footage of a Bangladeshi garment factory clearly using child workers. Glass was then asked on camera whether the young girl in the film should not be in school instead of sewing clothes for Wal-Mart. Predictably, he stammered out a "yes" before walking off the set. He would have served the debate better by pointing out that the reporter's was a very American question, geared to an American audience. An Asian audience would immediately recognize that the real alternative for that Bangladeshi girl would not be trundling off to class but scavenging through garbage heaps or prostituting herself.

And not just in Asia. During the Depression, when my paternal grandfather was out of work, my father supported the family with various jobs. None were as dire as that of the little girl in the Bangladeshi textile mill or required him to forgo his education, but the burden that fell on his shoulders then would probably seem appalling to his grandchildren today. In a sense, that's progress. And yet there are people in many countries who are faced with similar trade-offs: money saved by having a girl work in a factory may not only help feed her family but go toward educating a brother, who might ultimately find work that is financially more remunerative and thus support the whole family.

To our sensibilities, this is not an attractive trade-off. But in real life poor people typically do not have the choices we wish them to have, and the market sometimes brings better choices even when that is not its intention. While it might soothe Western consciences to "eliminate" child labor through regulations, in reality we may—if successful—be forcing children into something worse. This is not an argument "for" child labor. It does, however, posit that laws forbidding it will have the desired effect only where the culture and the overall market conditions support them. The history of most such regulation, moreover, suggests that the best hope for success lies largely in places where the economic necessity for the behavior being outlawed has largely disappeared and the law tends more to reflect than create social consensus.

Or take minimum wage laws. Undeniably a minimum wage does provide some workers with jobs with more money, at least assuming the society is law-abiding enough to respect those laws (even in our own rich country, look at how many people—for example, nannies—continue to work off the books). But if the minimum wage is set above the market wage, we are going to have, almost by definition, fewer jobs.

In not a few contexts, that can leave those in the social out-groups even worse off. History gives us many instances—for example, when white Western workers have skillfully deployed minimum wage laws to insulate themselves from competition from their yellow- and brown-skinned brothers.

South African whites understood this all too well. In 1919, the South African Mine Workers Union said that the "real point on that is that whites have been ousted by coloured labor. . . . It is now a question of cheap labour versus what is called 'dear labour,' and we will have to ask the commission to use the word 'colour' in the absence of a minimum wage, but when that [minimum wage] is introduced we believe that most of the difficulties in regard to the coloured question will drop out."[2] A variant of the same obtained in Australia, where the first plank of the Labor Party was "Australia for the white man" (which phrase for years adorned the weekly *Bulletin*, Australia's equivalent of *Newsweek*). Down under, the threat was not blacks but Asians, primarily Chinese. Accordingly, the

"White Australia" policy was born. White Australia was founded on the bedrock of restrictive immigration laws aimed at Asian immigration. But the White Australia policy was undergirded by more general labor laws to support the white worker, through, for example, minimum wage laws and tariffs. Although these laws were universal, their purpose was to support whites by insulating them from competition from Asian workers.

As Billy Hughes, the Labor leader who would become prime minister, so notoriously put it: "Our chief plank, is, of course, a White Australia. There is no compromise about that! The industrious coloured brother has to go—and remain away." Note the key objection: not that nonwhite workers were lazy but that they were "industrious."[3] It was for similar reasons that W. E .B. DuBois said that labor unions, which were notorious for not admitting blacks, were the "greatest enemy" of the black working man.

The same, incidentally, can be said for "safety" standards. Who could be against safety? Ask the Mexicans. As these words are written, a United States promise to open our highways to Mexican truckers has been stalled for years by efforts to ban Mexican-registered trucks on the grounds that they pose a threat to U.S. safety and environmental standards, an effort backed by American labor unions. Never mind that most of the long-haul trucks the Mexicans would use would have to pass U.S. emissions standards and be American-made.

Environmental concerns, of course, are legitimate. But what has happened to Mexican truckers and their families shows that a high-sounding purpose can easily mask crass self-interest. And when it comes to getting the government to intervene to help, poor Mexican workers are not likely to be a match for wealthy American environmentalists and their allied union lobbyists. Not least of the reasons to fear government regulation designed to achieve specific outcomes is that the outcomes are more likely to favor the wealthy and politically connected than the truly down and out.

Finally Rebecca mentioned discrimination. Let me again relate this to the developing world, where the stakes are so much higher. Back in the 1950s, the Philippines was not the economic basket case we know today; back then its economy was second only to Japan's. And in the guise of preventing foreign multinationals (mostly Americans and Japanese) from discriminating against Filipinos in their own country, Manila passed a series of laws limiting what foreigners could own. The government called this the "Filipino First" policy, which President Garcia in 1960 described as "an honest to goodness effort of the Filipino people to be master of their own economic household."[4] To this day the laws intended to ensure that Filipinos enjoyed a piece of the economic pie in their own land still operate to exclude the country's sizeable ethnic Chinese from direct ownership of a host of industries, which they get around by paying Filipinos to front for them. The result of trying to ensure a fair shake for Filipinos ended up creating fat, exploitative oligopolies that enrich the well-connected while keeping the general populace impoverished.

So, yes, I am skeptical about government. And not simply because of a Ronald Reaganish belief that government tends to be inefficient even in the best cases. Efficiency is one thing, but when it comes to morality the more operative concern I have is that when the government intervenes, it puts the powers of the state on the side of one interest—which makes redress much more difficult to effect. That is what made Jim Crow so pernicious in the South: Not only could those who wanted to discriminate count on custom and prejudice, they had the whole machinery of the state behind them as well, leaving African Americans with no real options.

Rebecca, of course, is as much against unwise and ineffective regulations as I am. But that's the whole issue: if it were as easy to do as Rebecca implies, our problems would have been solved long ago. Indeed, I wish that the people so eager to address "market failure" could bring themselves to address "government failure." Look how long it took the United States to pass welfare reform, even after decades of experience attested to the devastation and dependency that it created in African American family life.

Thus far I have spoken only about those areas in which government intervenes to tame the market. But I am even more dubious (if that's possible!) about so-called positive interventions. That is because, as I alluded to in my initial essay, the opposite of competition is not cooperation. It is collusion.

Let me again limit myself to Rebecca's examples, because it seems to me she judges these interventions not by their actual outcomes but by their intentions. She cites education, in one sense a perfect example: with rare exceptions, even private education at almost all levels—elementary, high school, university—enjoys much public support and subsidy. But let us focus on the system in which the government is most involved and in which most Americans are in fact educated: the public education system.

Let me concede that for the majority of white Americans, or at least the majority of suburban public schools, this system works reasonably well. But if ever there were an instance of government failure on a massive scale, our urban school systems would head the list. And when that failure is broken down by race, it assumes probably the biggest civil rights indictment of our age.

According to the National Association for Educational Progress—"the nation's report card"—nearly two-thirds of African American and Hispanic fourth-graders cannot read at grade level. What makes the fourth grade so telling is that the evidence indicates that a child who is not reading or performing at grade level by then probably never will—and the national high school dropout rates confirm that prediction. In any economy that would be a tremendous economic and social problem. But in an economy such as ours, which places an increasing premium on know-how, it means that the public school system is effectively writing out the majority of Hispanic and black children from a real shot at the American Dream as early as the age of ten or eleven.

Is it not true that even Harvard enjoys public subsidies without that kind of harm? Well, yes, but that rather begs the point. There is no doubt that government intervention has been the least debilitating in private universities, which is only to say that government damages less where it governs least. It is not simply a function of dollars either. In the District of Columbia, the per-pupil expenditure of $12,000 ranks among the highest in the nation, yet academic performance is among the lowest: Not only do D.C. students underperform, the longer they stay in the public schools the dumber they seem to get. Which is why, as a rule, those of us who in principle favor less government involvement are the same people pushing hardest for giving poorer minority students the choices in education that their wealthier white counterparts have.

Or take the U.S. Postal Service, which Rebecca cites as an example of an effective government service that has survived even in the face of new competition from, for example, UPS or FedEx. I am not sure that if I were arguing Rebecca's side I would be inclined to bring up the post office, which now appears on the General Accounting Office's list of "high-risk" organizations in financial crisis.[5] Not only does the post office exist only as a function of political patronage—it continues in its present fix because few members of Congress are willing to go on record as voting for a much-needed reduction in the jobs-rich processing centers—it has used its public subsidies and privileges (no taxes!) to drive other legitimate players from the scene. Talk to the owner of a passport photo service in California who saw his business drop dramatically when the post office started competing with him. Or talk to the others on the electronic frontier who fear that, not content with losing millions each year on sorting regular mail, the post office will start poaching their territories from a government-protected vantage point.

Finally, in terms of "positive" interventions Rebecca cites Asia. Without doubt, Asia's growth over the past four decades cannot be attributed to "unfettered markets." Most are variations on the Japanese model of state-guided capitalism, albeit to differing degrees, with, as Rebecca puts it, "government incentives that encouraged local industry and made foreign investment attractive; . . . subsidies that encouraged education, increasing the productive skills of the population; and . . . astute diplomacy that created political connections that in turn smoothed economic connections."

Exactly. That was also the recipe for the corruption and inefficiency and rank favoritism that were so exposed during the Asian financial crisis. Asian peoples, moreover, know it. Not only do the more classically open economies such as Hong Kong boast a higher per capita GDP than the interventionist economies of, say, Korea and Indonesia, if you look them up on Transparency International's corruption scale you will see that the freer and more open the market, the less corruption. That is not because the people of Hong Kong are more personally virtuous than, say, the people of Indonesia or Korea. It is primarily because they do not need the government to do their business.

This experience has confirmed my disinclination to rely on the state to supply or even, in many cases, to enforce a proper moral code. And here, at least, is a Catholic inclination that can cut across traditional left-right divisions: it was a point of pride in Dorothy Day's Catholic Worker movement that it would not accept government money.

I want to be clear. I do not mean that the state has no place, even in areas like child labor, which I mentioned earlier. To get back to my traffic analogy about people obeying red lights even in the middle of the night (by the way, a very American, and, in my view, attractive American characteristic), the point was not that it obviated the need for police and laws. It is just that if police and laws are the *only* or even the primary means of ensuring that people obey, traffic would break down. If you think that is an exaggeration, you haven't been in a Manila traffic jam.

In my view the right ordering of economies functions likewise. To put it another way, it is hard enough, even in the best circumstances, for the government to do the basic things (coining money, upholding the rule of law, and so forth) without gumming up the works. Law works best when it ratifies some social consensus; it works least well when it tries to impose such a consensus—especially in the teeth of clear economic incentives against it.

Not that this lets me off the moral hook. For those of us who believe that markets are not morally self-sustaining, ruling out government only makes the imperatives of moral undergirding the more daunting. That is especially true for those of us whose Christian view of life tells us we cannot be neutral regarding certain individual choices. Rebecca maintains that economic actors are not simply passive, and no better example exists than the drug trade: though I oppose the legalization of drugs, it is difficult not to acknowledge that the economic incentives of the drug business loom so large that they seem to overwhelm not only the laws but any sense of individual or social restraint.

So what's a market Christian to do? The only honest answer lies in the culture. It is not an easy answer. Let me start with one of those infamous encyclicals: *Centesimus Annus*, the most market-friendly of all Catholic documents and the starting point for the Catholic debate over the parameters of a moral economic order. Many people read this, incorrectly, as a sort of warmed-over Catholic "third way," the idea that the debate is over the extent and degree of some welfare net. I incline to the view of Cardinal Avery Dulles, who says its principle message "bears not on politics and economics in themselves but rather on culture as the sustainer of both."[6]

I know: talk of culture can sound vague and gooey. But without culture, all is lost. For it is culture that determines the boundaries within which the market must operate and beyond which the market dare not go. These are not questions that can be reduced to the market's own yardstick of efficiency. Doubtless Rebecca and I both would concede that if trade in drugs, prostitution, or babies were made legal, the market would soon provide them more efficiently than the alternatives that now exist. None of these are markets Rebecca or I or probably the majority of Americans desire. But people can be and are used as if they were commodities. In some ways that is just what black markets do.

Oscar Wilde once quipped that "as long as war is regarded as wicked it will always have its fascinations. When it is looked upon as vulgar, it will cease to be popular." A flip remark, yes—but a backhanded testament to the power of culture to override the power of force. It is far easier, I concede, to assert the need for a rightly ordered culture than to get one. But that is the imperative from which there is no escape, at least for Christians who believe that human beings cannot be whole without their most important institutions tethered in some acknowledgment to transcendent truth.

In its most basic form, culture not only supplies the context within which markets operate, it also provides the institutions and values that no market can survive without. And though the caricature of the profit-maximizing individual is an assumption that even many market defenders make, the better economists recognize it for the one-dimensional crudity it is. As Gary Becker put it in his Nobel prize speech, "Along with others, I have tried to pry economists away from narrow assumptions about self-interest. Behavior is driven by a much richer set of values and preferences."[7] In other words, real human behavior can be as driven by altruism as by selfishness.

And it is here that the Christian indictment of libertarianism is most potent. For it simply makes no sense for a profit-maximizing individual to sacrifice him- or herself for another, much less for society. It is not so much that you cannot show that a libertarian might decide to risk his life following a rational calculation of the cost and benefits of defending his country. It is that this is simply a perverse way at looking at what most people consider a moral obligation, not a question of personal costs and benefits.

The point is that we have probably not paid enough attention to the social virtues without which a free market is impossible. Typically market defenders focus on the individual virtues upon which markets are founded. As Francis Fukuyama notes, however, "a strong argument can be made that the social virtues are prerequisites for the development of individual virtues like the work ethic, since the latter can be best cultivated in the context of strong groups—families, schools, workplaces—that are fostered in societies with a high degree of social solidarity."[8]

Again, in the third world the interplay between culture and state and economics tends to put the issue in higher relief. In China—which is undeniably getting richer as it opens its markets—old vices, from prostitution and drug use to the gross exploitation of workers, have once again reappeared. And nobody who knows China would ever believe that the government is going to be the one to solve these problems. In most parts of the third world, governments are always strong enough to foul things up but rarely up to the task of enforcing a rule of law.

This is precisely where John Paul's language about culture has the most to offer. Even in *Centesimus Annus*, where he detailed the failures of socialism and protectionism, he was careful to frame this not as a failure of economics but as a failure of anthropology—by which he meant a failure that was predestined because socialism was a system founded on a false understanding of man. This emphasis is underscored even more literally by the pope's favorite metaphor: the Culture of Death and the Culture of Life. Implicit in the pope's writings is the idea that an authentic human culture can never be completely rationalistic: it depends on nurturing premodern human institutions and understandings. Ironically, Fareed Zakaria makes much the same point about liberal democracy.[9]

Today it is common for Christians to see culture as opposed to their beliefs, and there is more than some truth in that if popular culture is what they mean. But Christians in the past have faced more than equal challenges. Put it this way: Would Britain ever have committed itself to the abolition of the slave trade without the culture-transforming work of John Wesley and William Wilberforce? Would the ascendancy of Abraham Lincoln and the Republican Party have been possible absent the coalition of antislavery Evangelicals and free labor advocates who believed that slavery was underwriting a system that would choke off opportunity to the new class of American workers? Closer to our time, did anyone who in 1979 watched a Polish pope address the crowd at St. Peter's Square even dream that the Berlin Wall might be breached a decade later?

Why do we underrate culture? Two reasons occur to me. First is that culture is a less direct and therefore less initially satisfying approach to social problems. Look at Enron. How much easier it is to prosecute a few bad guys (some of whom do deserve prosecution) and pass the Sarbanes-Oxley bill, which, only months after its passing, almost everyone admits had far more to do with politics than ethics. How much harder the task of creating a culture that would be far less accommodating of the find-the-loophole ethos of our Enrons, Tycos, WorldComs, and so forth.

In Euclidian geometry, the shortest distance between here and there is a straight line, but in the nexus between markets and morality (or between politics and morality) that doesn't hold. In fact, there is a strong argument to be made that the more regulations that exist, the more people feel that they have discharged their moral obligations by meeting a checklist. That is why regulations so often fail—because in the real world it is the lawyers who determine how they are enforced, and in the corporate world the more such regulations there are, the more pro forma efforts are made to comply, not to solve the problem but to reduce one's legal liabilities.

It helps to understand that in the Christian liberal tradition (a very different beast from the liberal Christian tradition), liberty has been defined as Lord Acton did: not as "the power of doing what we like, but the right of being able to do what we ought." That conception runs smack up against a marked tendency in contemporary society to define freedom as simply the expansion of choices with no reference to the value of those choices. In *Evangelium Vitae*, Pope John Paul referred to it as a "notion of freedom that exalts the isolated individual in an absolute way,"[10] to the point that we today, like Cain before us, do indeed react with some astonishment to any implication that we might be our brother's keeper. The point is that if freedom is defined solely as individuals being able to maximize their happiness through expanding choices, everyone else, far from being considered essential to their happiness, quickly becomes a potential threat to individual freedom.

So what are the distinctly social virtues we need to counter these trends, to make society safe for capitalism and democracy? The church has long insisted, first, on subsidiarity: the idea that the mediating institutions and authorities must be at the lowest workable level—that is, those closest to the people—rather than at the highest. In many ways that parallels Americans' republican understandings about government, reflected in the fascinating interplay of layers (local, county, state, federal) that are so natural in the United States that we give them no thought and so alien everywhere else that other people have incredible difficulty understanding them. There is nothing specifically Catholic about subsidiarity except the language, and though it may seem to be nothing more than common sense in a modern, rationalistic state, society tends to operate in the other direction, by imposing a solution (law or regulation) from the top down rather than building from the bottom up.

The other virtue, made more explicit by Pope John Paul II, is solidarity. Obviously the term has its origins in the movement in his native Poland, which not only helped usher in the end of communism but also united its citizens in an extraordinary sense of kinship. Tocqueville called religion America's "first political institution" for similar reasons, because he thought that religion and its attendant institutions tempered the nation's individualist impulses and prevented it from being consumed by selfishness. Solidarity encompasses a similar social ideal: a recognition that we are more than individuals, that we have an obligation (however limited) to the common good in and of itself, not just because of what we get back out of it. The implication, unlike the regulatory approach, is that our obligations may include but are certainly not limited to the letter of the law. And certainly this virtue will find far more fertile soil for cultivation in a society whose people have internalized the Christian sense of communion.

No doubt there are those, perhaps Rebecca is one, who believe that looking to culture rather than law to ensure a just economic order is naïve. But I would reverse that: To me, the idea that laws can be imposed in the absence of a supporting culture is far more naïve—and dangerous. Let me use one of the most contentious issues of the day to illustrate what I mean: abortion.

I happen to be firmly pro-life, in that I accept my church's teaching that the aborting of an fetus is the taking of a human life and intrinsically evil. Yet I do not believe in prohibiting abortion through a constitutional amendment, in much the same way I do not believe in regulating the economy. It is not so much that I *oppose* pro-life amendments in principle; it is that I believe that in practice they are rather beside the point—not least because they won't work without the culture behind them. It is not simply a question of tactics, though it is my belief that the so-called incremental approach—of dealing with abortion not as an all-or-nothing proposition but instead in specifics, such as partial birth abortion, parental consent for minors, and so forth—is the tactically sounder approach. I also reject a constitutional amendment because in a free society we Christians bear a far graver responsibility, which cannot be answered by sloughing off our work on politicians. In reality we have no choice but the culture: Given the technology of a very advanced and prosperous abortion industry, even a national law outlawing abortions would hardly stop them. To change laws in any meaningful sense we must first do what Wilberforce and Wesley did in Britain over slavery: change minds. That is much the harder task, which is why both pro-choicers and pro-lifers in practice find it hard to resist the silver bullet approach: a constitutional amendment or Supreme Court decision that settles the abortion issue (as Dred Scott settled slavery?) once and for all. You might say that I view a constitutional amendment outlawing abortion as possible only in a society that essentially does not need it.

Yet even within this framework of markets and competition, there still remains plenty of room for redressing injustices and taking the side of the weak against the powerful. As the leaders of the developing world are well aware, one of the tremendous problems they face is first world protectionism that excludes them from our markets. Even Adam Smith fretted about the imbalance between workers and managers, that whereas the latter were able to organize, the former were not. The flaw in economic justice generally has to do with the idea that it can be dispensed. As Christians, we need to have confidence that justice will be better served by allowing ordinary men and women to realize their talents in an atmosphere of freedom bounded by laws designed to set boundaries rather than to proscribe every possible instance of undesired behavior. Regulations, which have a tendency to multiply as people find ways to get around them, seldom work as intended.

In short, theologians and economists need each other. Theologians and religiously informed activists need to have some grasp of how the economy really works if their critiques are to be taken seriously. Obversely, market economists, if they are not to succumb to the same self-destructive hubris as the socialists, need a religiously informed culture to remind them that economics is made for human beings and not vice versa.

The pope has said repeatedly that man's destiny is freedom, genuine freedom. We know, from the considered experience of the century past, that markets work better than control, that markets require law and not simply license, in short, that freedom works—and, if we are Christians, that it works not because it sanctions greed but because it is more in accord with our God-created human natures. To reduce this to a question purely about the degree of intervention is to treat it as a purely mechanical issue when it is much larger. Perhaps I have left the impression that regulating an economy into morality is bad because such an approach imposes too much on an economy. What I really believe is that that approach imposes far too little on us.

Notes

1. Gordon Fairclough, "Child Labour: It Isn't Black and White," *Far Eastern Economic Review* (March 7, 1996).

2. W. E. Williams, "W. H. Hutt and the Economics of the Colour Bar," *Journal of Labor Research*, vol. 18, no. 2 (April 1, 1997).

3. Australian Broadcasting Company, *One Hundred Years: The Australian Story*, transcript, episode 2, "Rise and Fall of White Australia" (Sydney, 2001).

4. William McGurn, "A Tale of Two Countries," *Reason*, vol. 26, no. 2 (June 1, 1994).

5. General Accounting Office, *High Risk Series: An Update* (Washington, January 2003).

6. Avery Dulles, "Centesimus Annus and the Renewal of Culture," *Markets and Morality*, vol. 2, no. 1 (Spring 1999). In this, Cardinal Dulles notes that the vision of a social order divided into three distinct but overlapping spheres—political, economic, and cultural, with culture having priority over the other two—is not original

to Pope John Paul II but is the theme of the Vatican II document "The Pastoral Constitution on the Church in the Modern World."

7. Gary S. Becker, "The Economic Way of Looking at Life," *Journal of Political Economy*, vol. 101 (June 1993), p. 383.

8. Francis Fukuyama, *Trust: The Social Virtues and the Creation of Prosperity* (Free Press, 1995), p. 48.

9. Fareed Zakaria, *The Future of Freedom: Illiberal Democracy at Home and Abroad* (Norton, 2003).

10. John Paul II, *Evangelium Vitae* (The Gospel of Life) (Vatican City, March 1995), paragraph 19.

CONTRIBUTORS

Rebecca M. Blank is dean of the Gerald R. Ford School of Public Policy, the Henry Carter Adams Collegiate Professor of Public Policy, and professor of economics at the University of Michigan. She previously served as senior staff economist on the Council of Economic Advisers under President George H. W. Bush and was appointed as a member of the Council of Economic Advisers during the Clinton administration. Her research focuses on the interaction of the macroeconomy, government antipoverty programs, and the behavior and well-being of low-income families. Her publications include *Social Protection vs. Economic Flexibility: Is There a Trade Off?*; *It Takes a Nation: A New Agenda for Fighting Poverty*; and numerous scholarly articles.

E.J. Dionne Jr. is a senior fellow in Governance Studies at the Brookings Institution and University Professor in Foundations of Democracy and Culture at Georgetown University. He is a syndicated columnist with the *Washington Post* Writers Group and a co-chair, with Jean Bethke Elshtain, of the Pew Forum on Religion and Public Life. Dionne is the author of *Why Americans Hate Politics* and *They Only Look Dead*, and he is editor or coeditor of several Brookings volumes: *Community Works: The Revival of Civil Society in America*; *What's God Got to Do with the American Experiment?*; *Bush v. Gore*; *Sacred Places, Civic Purpose*; and *United We Serve: National Service and the Future of Citizenship*.

KAYLA MELTZER DROGOSZ is a senior research analyst for the religion and civil society project at the Brookings Institution, where her research interests include ethics, political philosophy, and the public purposes of religion. She is a coeditor of *United We Serve: National Service and the Future of Citizenship* and a series editor for the Pew Forum Dialogues on Religion and Public Life. She received her degree from New College, Oxford University, continued her graduate studies in religion at Hebrew University, and received an MPA from the Maxwell School of Citizenship and Public Affairs at Syracuse University. She served previously with the policy office of United Jewish Communities and in the political section of the U.S. Mission to the United Nations.

JEAN BETHKE ELSHTAIN is the Laura Spelman Rockefeller Professor of Social and Political Ethics at the University of Chicago. She is a member of the National Commission for Civic Renewal and currently serves as chair of both the Council on Families in America and the Council on Civil Society; she also is co-chair, with E.J. Dionne Jr., of the Pew Forum on Religion and Public Life. Elshtain is the author of several books, including *Jane Addams and the Dream of American Democracy*; *Who Are We? Critical Reflections and Hopeful Possibilities*; *Democracy on Trial*; *Public Man, Private Woman: Women in Social and Political Thought*; and *Just War against Terror: The Burden of American Power in a Violent World*.

WILLIAM MCGURN is the *Wall Street Journal*'s chief editorial writer and a member of its editorial board. McGurn earned a bachelor's degree in philosophy from Notre Dame and a master's in journalism from Boston University. He began his journalism career in 1981 as an assistant managing editor for the *American Spectator*. He has served as managing editor of *This World Magazine*, editorial features editor of the *Wall Street Journal Europe*, deputy editor of the *Asian Wall Street Journal*'s editorial page, Washington bureau chief for *National Review*, and senior editor of the *Far Eastern Economic Review*. He is also a member of the President's Commission on White House Fellowships.

INDEX